IN SEARCH OF THE WHIP-POOR-WILL LOVE SONG

Charles Brookins Taylor Sr.

ISBN 979-8-89112-722-7 (Paperback)
ISBN 979-8-89112-723-4 (Digital)

Scriptures references:

1. Verses marked KJV are from the Holy Bible, King James Version.
2. Verses marked NIV are from the Holy Bible, New International Version.
3. Verses marked GNT are from the Holy Bible, Good News Translation.

Copyright information:

In Search of the Whip-poor-will Love Song, Reference ID# 910932
1. Live Recording, Whippoorwills Singing and Accompanying Friends: Copyright Registration Number: SRu 1-563-191, January 12, 2024; Author Charles B. Taylor, Sr.; Claimant: Charles B. Taylor, Sr., 1491 Linder RD., Butler, AL, 36904.
2. My Whippoorwill Love Song: Copyright Registration Number: PAu 4-209-617, January 29, 2024; Author Charles B. Taylor, Sr.: Claimant: Charles B. Taylor, Sr., 1491 Linder Rd., Butler, AL 36904.

Covenant Books
11661 Hwy 707
Murrells Inlet, SC 29576
www.covenantbooks.com

This book is dedicated with love to my father, the late Oscar Taylor Sr., and to my mother, the late Rosa Brookins Taylor, who taught me how to love God's creation and God, who gave every aspect of His Creation the ability to proclaim His glory, and to all my bird-watching friends and advocates.

CONTENTS

ACKNOWLEDGMENT

Thanks to all those who shared with me their lifelong experience of having heard the Whip-poor-will birds sing; some of whom had the rare occasions of seeing them. I thank them for their able assistance, suggestions, and loving encouragement and many others who inspired me along this writing journey.

Finally, I thank my publisher, Covenant Books Publishing Company, and its representatives and staff members who guided me through this process.

INTRODUCTION

In Search of the Whip-poor-will Love Song story reminds us that God uses all His creatures or things in His creation, each in His own unique way and each for a unique purpose, to declare or proclaim the glory of God. The Scripture teaches us that all the works of God have as their ultimate goal to display God's glory.

Although we have never seen God with our natural eyes, we can witness His mighty works in all His creations by observing the innumerable ways each part expresses it.

The whip-poor-will is no exception. God created it with its own uniqueness and for a unique purpose. It is a reminder that each creature or thing in God's creation has a purpose to fulfill and a role to play in the general scheme of existence. And He has given each of us and every other member of His creation the innate ability to accomplish an ordained purpose in relating to Him, each in its own unique way.

It is a reminder to us that God can use people or other members of His creation we may think are insignificant to do great things.

In the mindset of most people, in the past, and even in the present, the whip-poor-will is considered to be an insignificant bird who simply sings its name at night. And the rare pictures taken of it depict it as being less attractive than most other birds.

By and large, the whip-poor-will song with its haunting, and seemingly ethereal effect on its hearers, has been used in movies, novels, songs, or poems to convey a message of loneliness.

It is often used as an auditory symbol in the setting of rural America, depicting the whip-poor-will and its song as a symbol of evoking in us not only a sense of loneliness but also sadness and a feeling of not belonging as it penetrates our imaginative minds ceaselessly throughout most of the night from early spring to late summer.

However, we are going to discover as we read *In Search of the Whip-Poor-Will Love Song* that God can use people or things we may think or see as not being attractive or significant, or even as a nuisance in ways that encourage us to know that we are never alone and that we are loved. And each of us has the potential to do extraordinary things. Also we are going to discover that God is using the whip-poor-will to proclaim a message of love for us that is unconditional and unfailing.

The whip-poor-will's singing has been heard by many, yet it is said that less than 1 percent of the world's population has ever visually seen a whip-poor-will. Of course, one can easily understand this because it's a night bird and therefore is active at night. It is nocturnal. It sleeps during the day. No doubt, many of you, as me, have had to work the night shift. The whip-poor-will has been called by God to work on the night shift.

Birds in general are very popular. For example, each of our fifty states has a designated state bird. Currently, seven states designate the cardinal (red-jay bird) as its state bird. The mockingbird is second with five states designating it as their state bird. There are several reasons why the cardinal and mockingbird are the most popular. Visibility, year-round habitation, and perceived attractiveness are the main reasons. Yet the whip-poor-will, like every member of God's creation, is given a special purpose and a unique ability to carry out its function on earth. The whip-poor-will is assigned a special message to deliver. God gave it a love song to sing to each other and to us, in its own way, in its own language. And He gave it a special dance to dance.

It has been faithful to its calling; it has been singing its song since its very beginning. Like a circuit preacher, traveling from place to place in its proper seasons, it has been carrying out its God-given functions in life. It is a humble creature; it seeks no daylight fame. It is faithful to its God-given call to sing its all-important message in the solitude of darkness as a voice crying out—singing out in the night. It has been faithfully singing its love song, on cue, almost unceasingly every night beginning in the early spring nights and ending in the late summer. Yet we humans have failed to grasp the meaning and significance of its message. In part, it's because we have been subconsciously led to believe it is just another creature we think is too insignificant to have a real message, especially because it sings at night, as other birds occasionally do. And mistakingly we think if it can't be seen, but only heard, it must not have an important message for us to consider receiving.

We are told that man's primary purpose is to give glory to God. But let us not forget this includes the whole of God's creation.

"Let the whole earth be filled with His glory," writes the psalmist (Psalm 72:19). "The angels in heaven echo this same message as they uttered, the whole earth is full of his glory" (Isaiah 6:3).

In Psalm 19:1, we read, "the heavens declare the glory of God."

This is one of the clearest biblical statements that creation itself is meant to show the greatness of God. The psalmist goes on to say that there is no speech or language where God's ordained voice is not heard. And His speech is uttered day unto to day, and night unto night (Psalm 19:2–3). This means He is speaking to us twenty-four hours each day through every member of His creation; God's Word is spoken in some form or fashion night and day.

Although He has given us His written Word to speak to us, He also speaks to us through His visible and invisible creation. What is hindering our listening?

One reason we are not listening is because we are being taught, by and large, that we must separate the spiritual from the physical aspect of God's creation.

This concept is most prevalent in our western culture. In essence, we are being taught to consciously separate the spiritual from the physical by drawing an imaginary line between the two.

We have not fully understood that God's creation includes both the spiritual and physical aspects of existence.

It is true that He transcends His creation, yet He permeates both the spiritual and the natural realms. And He is constantly speaking in and through each.

What hinders us from hearing God speaking to us?

For one thing, in our society man is increasingly being inundated with man-made noises and voices making it more difficult for us to hear God speaking to us in the spiritual and physical realms.

In addition, we are spending more time indoors than outdoors. Also as we go outside, we are taking our man-made gadgetry that streams man-made voices and sounds, often accompanied by video images.

Notice that more and more people are listening to their radio or iPhones or talking on their car phones while they are driving. And even when we go outside to participate in outdoor activities, notice how many people are listening to their favorites, voices, and noises while wearing their headphones connected to their iPhones or some other means of communication. And as a result, we are being bombarded with incessant voices that are drowning out the voice of God as He speaks to us in the natural and spiritual realms. Regrettably we are becoming more and more oblivious to our surroundings and thereby becoming more and more disconnected with other people and God's creation outdoors.

This disconnection is increasingly causing us to become more and more oblivious to the beauty of God's creation and how He uses every aspect of His creation to speak to us. We all need to get outside more and intentionally get in tune with all of God's creation. And when you allow this to happen, your life will increasingly become more fulfilled and gracious.

We must not forget that we are made in the image of God, and we are the crown of His creation. He has made us stewards over all His creation, and we can only carry out this responsibility when we are in tune with and connected to every aspect of it. Moreover, we must also remember God created us as relational beings. We are to relate to God, others, and His entire creation.

Remember, as we become more attuned to God's creation all around us, we will begin to recognize that God has given the whole of His creation, and each one of us the ability to proclaim His glory in word and in deed and thereby become more relational in our response to God, others and the whole of His creation. Likewise, He has given each member of His creation, from the minutest of atoms to the largest sun, the tiniest amoeba to the greatest whale, and all things inestimable, in its own unique way the ability to speak to us.

All of God's creation speaks to us in its own language

It is important for us to remember that although all of God's creation speaks to us in its own language—in praise, proclamation, moans, and groans—however, to man, these utterings are mostly unintelligible, and not readily linguistically translated.

In reading this book, you are going to discover the whip-poor-will is not just an insignificant bird singing its name in the night.

The question I intend to answer is this: If the whip-poor-will is not singing its song, what is it singing? Over the years, some have suggested it is singing its name, "Whip-poor-will." Some have suggested it is singing, "Chip fell out the oak tree." Others have even suggested it is singing "Whip her or I will" or some other utterings.

As you journey with me, you and I will discover how the advancement of technology will increasingly help us linguistically translate and interpret different languages and the song of the whip-poor-will in ways we can better understand.

What is that message? It is this writer's belief that it is a love song anchored in God, flowing from God with a twofold purpose: First, it is a love song from God reminding us He loves us. Second, it is a love song from God to us through the whip-poor-will and to each other.

Moreover, God is using the whip-poor-will to remind us He wants to use each one of us to be a conduit through which His unconditional love can flow.

It is my hope as you journey with me, it will encourage you to take time out from the hustle and bustle of life and be still and know that God is God (Psalm 46:10). Be still and listen to God speak to us through the whip-poor-will with a message of love. Be still and learn to appreciate the beauty of God's creation by joining me on the quest searching for the whip-poor-will love song. And in doing so, you will learn more about the whip-poor-will and how God uses it in a very special way.

It is my hope that as you read this book, you will be encouraged to appreciate the beauty of God's creation and how He can use every member of His creation, each in its own unique way.

This is a wonderful truth I have discovered, and in doing so, it has increasingly helped me in my daily quest in my understanding the meaning and purpose of my life. The more I learned about the whip-poor-will, the more I learned that God has given it and each member of His creation a language to speak, a song to sing, and a dance to dance.

And it is important for us to remember that each one of us as members of humankind has also been given by God a language to speak, a song to sing, and a dance to dance.

As you journey with me via the characters in this book, it is my prayer that God will remind you that He is using the whip-poor-will in a special way, and likewise, He wants to use you in a special way.

In my quest in writing *In Search of the Whip-Poor-Will Love Song*, I intend to answer the following questions:

1. Who or what is this bird called the whip-poor-will?
2. Is it just singing its name or is it singing a love song?
3. Is it a gift from God?
4. For whom it is meant?
5. And, what is its love song saying?

Whip-poor-will

Drawing by: Charles Brookins Taylor, Sr.

CHAPTER 1

The Background and the Setting

As we journey in our search for the whip-poor-will love song, it is important to show how key background information such as the generational setting—social, economical, environmental, technology, and our value system inform our search in each succeeding generation.

**The background setting emanating from
the GI generation—1900–1945**

The setting is in Choctaw County, in southwestern Alabama, near the Mississippi borderline. The central location is a little town called Butler, Alabama, near the Tombigbee River, where the Choctaw and Chickasaw Indians used to roam. The region is ideal for the whip-poor-will to carry out its function in life. The temperature is ideal, plentiful forestry for ideal habitation, and the insects are plentiful.

Even today Alabama is about 70 percent forest land densely covered with undergrowth that provides a perfect setting for the whip-poor-will and other wildlife habitation. And we can safely surmise in saying it was even more densely covered during the GI generation. In part, because little or no pesticides or other chemicals were used during this period.

Remember, during this generation, Alabama's main industry was farming. The setting was ideal for whip-poor-will habitation with its many open fields scattered throughout the wooded terrain. In addition, its small towns were sparsely scattered throughout the predominantly rural area, many with inadequate roads to travel to and from each other. And yes, many were without access to electricity.

And of course, this favored the whip-poor-will, a night bird, in that darkness was more wide spread, due to the fact there was less light pollution, resulting from not having the availability of many man-made sources of artificial light as today.

Also remember, Benjamin Franklin discovered electricity in 1752; however, even in the early 1900s many, especially those in the rural areas, did not have access to electricity.

Additionally, Henry Ford produced the first Model T Ford in 1908. The first international tractor was built in 1906. Henry Ford is credited for introducing the first assembly line which influenced mass production. It was the beginning of the industrialization of America, the beginning of technological advancement that would evolve more rapidly through each succeeding generation.

However, during the GI generation, 1900–1925, farmers still predominantly relied mostly on the horse, the mule, the wagon, and an assortment of plows and other cultivating tools. The horse and buggy was still being used by those who could not afford the luxury of a Model T Ford.

With this in mind, one can easily understand there was less noise pollution, again ideal for the whip-poor-will.

I am sure if the whip-poor-will could speak to us today above and beyond singing its song, it would happily agree: Those were surely the *good old days*, years ago. These were the economical, environmental, and social settings in which Samuel and Anne, the father and mother of David, lived.

A close-up look at the setting in which Samuel and Anne lived

Samuel and Anne lived a few miles west of Tombigbee River in Choctaw County, near a little town that is today called Butler,

Alabama. Samuel was born in the days when many like him, especially boys, had to drop out of school by the time they reached the fourth grade. During the GI generation, oftentimes this was a result of having to start work at an early age for the family to survive.

It was a time when farming was the main source of income and food. Needless to say, the larger the family, the more feasible it was to have a large farm. In fact, the size of the family usually dictated the size of the farm operated by the family. Also, families who did not have farms rented out their labor to other farmers and related labor forces.

Formal education was not a top priority during this generation. In order to obtain a job, essentially the ability to exhibit common sense and do manual labor that required certain degrees of physical ability and the ability to follow instructions were the primary requirements.

We must remember farming is very demanding. Farming requires year-round attention. And the working hours are from sunup to sundown. It is controlled by the seasons of the year. Soil preparation, seed planting, cultivation, and harvesting must be done in a timely manner. It takes year-round vigilance.

During this era, by the time a boy reached the age of eight, he was considered to be mentally and physically able to work on a farm with little or no supervision. This was the social and economical setting that Samuel grew up in. And so, it was not unusual for a boy to drop out of school at the age of ten.

Whereas Anne was able to complete twelve years of schooling which was more common for girls to do so during this generation. This was in part made possible because the girls, with few exceptions, were mostly relegated to take care of the home affairs and therefore were not required to do extended farm work as were the boys.

It was typical during this time and period that a girl who had a twelfth-grade education often was qualified to become a teacher. Such was the case with Anne.

Anne was able to teach in one of the few schools in her region, oftentimes, in a one-room-school house which was typical during this time and period.

Samuel and Anne had known each other since first grade. As years passed, and as they grew older, they became more and more fond of each other and began dating.

Samuel, as he grew older, was able to work on jobs outside his family farming, and in addition to inheriting his family property, he was soon able to purchase additional land.

By now Samuel and Anne had developed a strong love relationship, and as the years went by, his hinting that he wanted to marry her became stronger.

And the action he had shown in preparing for marriage demonstrated that he was serious about getting married and raising a family. For example, at age twenty-two, in addition to the farmland and two houses he had inherited from his parents, and as a result of hard work, he was also able to purchase another two hundred acres of timberland and farmland.

His action left no doubt that he was serious about preparing a place for them to live and one day raise a family. Oh course, Anne also knew by getting married, she would be required to limit her teaching and increasingly become a full-time housewife.

At age twenty-two, Samuel was able to pop the big question: "Will you marry me?" Anne said yes.

Samuel, at age twenty-two, and Anne, at the age of twenty-one, were married, and their journey together as a family began. In the span of eleven years, they birthed five children. David was the fifth child. David stood out from the other children, not because he was seen as better than the others, but because his special interest in animals of all sorts, especially birds, did not go unnoticed. And naturally this meant that he loved being outdoors and had developed a keen interest for the whip-poor-will and the song it sings.

Why those who live on a farm are more readily exposed to wildlife, especially the whip-poor-will

Looking at the social, environmental, and economical settings and surroundings in which Samuel and Anne's family lived gives us an excellent example of why those who live on a farm have more exposure to wildlife, especially the whip-poor-will.

By the time David had reached the age of six, Samuel and Anne's family had accumulated more than three hundred acres of land. They now had a diversified group of farming entities: timber, cotton, corn, wheat, sweet potatoes, pecan orchards, fruit orchards, cattle raising, pig raising, and horses and mules, and an assortment of equipment and buildings necessary for operating these various farm activities.

And aside from this, we must not forget Anne always had her special garden where she grew vegetables and beautiful flowers for the entire family and community.

In addition to his family of seven sharing in operating the farm business, Samuel also hired workers from outside the family.

Clearly, he was not just a farmer, but he was also a businessman who provided jobs for many others. His family business, alone with providing income for his family, and jobs for others, also produced food and farm-related resources for the surrounding communities, both near and far.

Samuel was blessed with a keen sense of business and lots of energy and vitality, and it goes without saying, that he was one of the hardest-working men from both far and near. And he made sure that his children were hard workers too.

Samuel had a saying that forever stuck in David's memory: "If you want to be a businessman, you got to be willing to work hard."

David remembered upon hearing his father say this, he would ask a rhetorical question within himself: "Is this what being a businessman means?"

Years later, David would say, "After I became an adult and entered into the world of work, it didn't take me long to discover the answer to that question. The answer is yes." And even years later, David would agree that his experience on the farm taught him to appreciate the dignity of work and the beauty of God's creation.

First and foremost, however, Samuel and his family were faithful Christians and had grown to realize that God was the source of all their blessings. By living on a farm, they became more and more aware that living on a farm, even in the midst of constant activity, they believed they were closer to God and His creation than anywhere else. And because of this, they had the opportunity to be exposed to the outdoors and its many wildlife habitat, including the whip-poor-will and its singing at night. Yet in the midst of all the necessary farming activities, they felt a sense of peace and serenity beyond explaining.

In the midst of constant activities taking place on Samuel and Anne's farm, there is also a constant presence of peace and serenity

As indicated earlier, Alabama has one of the highest percentages of forest land in the United States, approximately 70 percent—the many varieties of trees, shrubberies, and flowers, including wildflowers and undergrowth and other competing vegetation, many of which produce seeds for the birds and other wildlife year-round.

Also remember, Butler, Alabama, which is near the Tombigbee River, is located on the cusp of the subtropical climate, approximately one hundred miles north of the Gulf Shores. This, too, is a factor that helps to maintain an ideal climate for growing fruits and vegetables almost year-round.

With all the many varieties of trees, shrubberies, flowers, and the multitude of other competing vegetation shedding its leaves, etc., which goes back into the ground, feeding it with rich nutrients through the process of natural decay and fermentation, it's no wonder that Alabama has some of the riches soil in the world.

This is the environmental setting in which Samuel's and Anne's farm and home lie in. Although there are constant activities going on during the day, when night comes, there is calmness and a sense of peace and tranquility one cannot explain.

Think about it: as night approaches, the cows, horses, chickens, hogs, and most wildlife animals cease their routine activities and begin taking their regular trips along the familiar sunbaked, foot-trodden clay paths, and as they travel to their place of resting at night, the birds routinely fly to their designated places of nesting at night.

In addition, the domesticated cats and dogs travel to their respective places to rest at night. Of course, the cats are nocturnal; therefore, nighttime is their favorite time to do their prowling ventures.

Likewise, human activities outdoors begin to cease as they, too, go to their places of abode. All is quiet except the night singing birds, especially the whip-poor-will.

A time for Samuel and his family's evening supper

Anne and the three girls in the family have finished preparing supper, and the round dining table has been set with lots of food. Samuel and the three boys have finished their final outdoor activities for the day. Each member of the family has a role to play, each one joining together for the common good of all.

Now it is time to eat. As usual, the family gathers around the round-shaped dining room table. Each one sits in his or her mutually designated chair; the usual prayer and blessing of the food takes place; each one is given an opportunity to share with each other their daily concerns. Oh, how we long for this type of family connectedness today!

Now for a brief wind-down time on the
front porch, first things first

By now, all the animals have ceased their usual noise, and the day birds have hushed their singing; all is quiet. It was wind-down time.

Wind-down time is a time for Samuel and Anne to put first things first. On this particular evening, they had the front porch all to themselves. Once again it was time to put first things first, no matter how hectic the day has been.

As they smilingly focus their eyes on each other, it is a special time to again say, "I love you." Over the years, they have learned it is not good enough to assume they love each other simply because they are together; it is important to tell each other with words. There are times when the words we speak are more important than what we do. As they held hands and looked into each other eyes, they both uttered the all-important words: "I love you."

With this sweet and solemn assurance, they were now contented with just sitting there obliviously staring out into open space, occasionally whispering to each other as the sweet fragrance of the roses, and other assortment of flowers and trees and competing vegetation permeated the evening air as it came sweeping in with its soft southern breeze, caressing their faces.

A rare opportunity for Samuel and Anne: getting a rare chance to see two whip-poor-wills engaging in a brief courting and dancing routine

Remember what was said earlier: Less than 1 percent of the world's population has ever seen a whip-poor-will, but many have heard them singing what appears to be their name.

However, this time of the year, early spring, over the years, during Samuel's and Anne's routine of sitting on the front porch for wind-down time after supper, it was also a time that gave them the opportunity to hear the whip-poor-will sing a song that appeared to be a message of love.

Early spring had already arrived weeks earlier in southwest Alabama. It is now early April. The whip-poor-wills have arrived.

The temperature is ideal. Insects and other food sources that the whip-poor-will feeds on are increasing day by day.

The camellia evergreen trees are now in full bloom with its beautiful red rose-like flowers. The Carolina creeping vines with its white trumpet-shaped flowers had reached its peak form. The early sprouts of spring grass and weeds are rapidly peeping above the ground.

The moon is in its waxing stages: moving from its first crescent toward the full-moon phase. There's something about the moon that causes the whip-poor-will to intensify its singing as the moon phase goes from the first crescent to its full-moon phase. Likewise, whether we know it or not, the phases of the moon affect all of us and all living things including the water tides in some way, either directly or indirectly. In fact, scientists say the moon phases affect all of creation in ways many or not fully aware of.

On this particular evening, Samuel and Anne are about to get a *once-in-a-lifetime* opportunity to witness a male and female whip-poor-will courting and dancing.

On this quiet April evening, as Samuel and Anne sit on the front porch as part of their daily routine during their usual evening wind-down time, they became a member of the less than 1 percent club reserved for those who have ever seen a whip-poor-will close-up.

The setting was ideal for this to happen as their house was located in an area near the garden that had been recently cultivated and seeded with variety of vegetable plants, and most of all, the soil was soft and loose with its sandy loam topsoil, ideal for the whip-poor-will and other birds including chickens to daily dust bathe as they flutter their wings back and forth to sift the sand throughout their feathers, in part to help get rid of parasites.

Now that they had taken their dust bathe, it was time to peck in the sand with its grit and fine gravel and swallow it to be used in their gizzard to aid in the process of digesting their food. (More will be said about this in chapter 6).

For now, let's get back to the exciting and rare glimpse of male and female whip-poor-wills in their courtship and dancing routine.

The porch where they sat was just a stone's throw away from one of their gardens. This was an ideal time for Samuel and Anne to spend quiet time alone, albeit sometimes the kids would join them on the porch, especially David, the youngest child. However, on this particular evening, David was not with them.

A once-in-a-lifetime scene: witnessing whip-poor-wills' courting and dancing scene

The scene that Samuel and Anne were about to witness was a reminder that some special moments come once in a lifetime. Like the most beautiful multicolored bird that flew by your bedroom window early one spring morning that you never saw again. It is a reminder that sometimes a special blessing only comes once; therefore, we must always be ready to seize the moment.

On this late summer evening, Samuel and Anne were all alone, or so they thought. Suddenly, they heard what sounded like slow-popping corn. As they looked toward the garden nearby, they saw what appeared to be a bird that looked like what one would call a quail (bobwhite, or a nighthawk, or a whip-poor-will). For many years, these three birds have been confused with one another. However, it dawned on them what they had heard others say: the whip-poor-will begins their movement just before the night shadows overcome the daylight.

The daylight was beginning to give way to darkness. Suddenly they noticed a movement taking place in the garden nearby. It was a female whip-poor-will waddling and fluttering her wings, sifting the sand throughout her feathers, on a sandy road near the garden. They now noticed that a male whip-poor-will was landing near the female whip-poor-will who was enjoying her dust bath.

As a result, the female whip-poor-will while remaining in the same location began moving her body up and down by squatting down and raising up on her short legs as high as possible. At the same time, she was shivering or pulsating her wings. The male began a slow dance movement, advancing a step at a time toward its mate. Next, he began raising his body, using the full length of his short legs at each step while making a swaying or wavering movement.

The female whip-poor-will, now with her head lowered, and her wings and tail outspread began a sidestepping dance back and forth; then half way around (180 degrees) to the right, and then back to the left while, at the same time, making a curious guttural chuckle.

The male continued his dance entirely around the female, swaying, while moving his body up and down by raising up high on his legs and then lowering his body as he bent his legs. The dance routine ended with the male bird turning toward the female bird as she turned toward him, both touching each other's bill.

The scene ended with the male and female whip-poor-will birds fading into the darkness as they moved into the woods nearby. The whole scene took about two minutes.

Shortly, thereafter the whip-poor-wills began singing their whip-poor-will love song nearby. This memorable and rare scene will never be forgotten by Samuel and Anne.

CHAPTER 2

A Visionary Dream That Will Never Be Forgotten by Samuel

By now, all the children had gone into their rooms for the night. Now it was time for Samuel and Anne to retire to bed. It was a night that Samuel and Anne would never forget, and they would tell it to their children, and others, over and over again.

After saying goodnight to Anne, Samuel quickly dozed off to sleep. Soon, his sleep evolved into a beautiful dream. In his visionary dream, he saw a picture of the whip-poor-wills courting and dancing in what appeared to be picture-perfect light.

In the background, he saw beautiful mountainous streams of water cascading from the sky. In each direction he looked, he saw skies painted with rainbow colors that presented the most pictur-esque skies he had ever seen.

Coupled with this was the symphonic sound of the sweetest music that he had ever heard ringing from all around. And at the same time the whip-poor-wills were dancing, there also appeared angelic beings in the background, dancing and singing to the beat of the music.

The song that the angelic beings were singing did not appear to be singing the name of "whip-poor-will." Rather, Samuel heard words that included something about love being real.

Not only was it the most beautiful scene he had ever witnessed, but it was also the most beautiful music he had ever heard. It was a glorious scene beyond that which words cannot fully describe. Surely, it left an indelible imprint on Samuel's memory that would never leave him, one which he would always share with those close to him.

When morning came, Samuel awoke from sleep. And of course, that morning at the breakfast table with the entire family present, he shared his dream with them. As he was telling what he had heard and seen in his visionary dream to his family, it was so touching that you could hear a *pin drop.*

Needless to say, from then on, Samuel's family, upon hearing the whip-poor-will sing at night, the song as well as the whip-poor-will itself took on a new meaning.

Interlude: The day that the howling of the coyotes cut David's fishing trip short

As indicated before, David loved the outdoors. Over the years, it was not unusual for his curiosity to lead him into adventures that caused the rest of the family, especially his mother, to have concerns for his safety.

No doubt, many of you, as I, have heard the old saying, "Curiosity killed the cat." By nature, young people, especially boys, take more chances in life adventures because they too often think they are invincible. With this mindset, David often went hunting for squirrels, rabbits, and so on, and as a result, he often found himself wandering deep into the backwoods all alone.

One of David's pastime activities was his love for fishing. One incident that stood out was the time he went fishing alone in his favorite fishing spot, which was a short distance from his family home.

It was late one early spring afternoon; David took his fishing pole, burlap sack, and bait, along with his fishing box, which included a knife, extra bobbers, sinkers, and assorted hooks, and quietly snuck off alone and headed to his favorite fishing spot.

Only minutes after he threw his line into the creek and began fishing, the fish started biting. As a result, he caught several fish within fifteen minutes.

Suddenly, an early spring shower passed over, bringing with it a rain shower that lasted not more than ten minutes (which is typical in this subtropical climate). The raindrops, as they bounced off the creek water, excited the fish even more. Now David was able to land several more pan-size catfish, along with bluegills.

As he casually glanced up at the sky, he noticed that the clouds had nearly passed over, and now he could see a full moon dimly shining as it rose from the east. After noticing that he had caught nearly two dozen fish, more than enough for a meal for everyone in the family, he quickly put them in a burlap sack and secured it with a piece of heavy-duty fishing line.

He was so excited, so much so, until he had forgotten that it was almost dark. And as a result of the rain showers, he was almost soaking wet as his clothing was steaming from moisture evaporating from his warm body. David said to himself, "How the time passes when you are having fun."

But David also knew by now his mother was wondering where he was. He had the urge to throw his fishing line back into the water just one more time before finally packing up and heading home.

Suddenly, he heard what sounded like wild coyotes howling nearby with their familiar sound, "*Eoo-hoho-hoo. Eoo-hoho-hoo.*" He was not sure whether they were howling at the full moon or howling at him. One thing is for sure, he did not wait around to find out. He quickly gathered his fishing equipment and fish. It was amazing how the adrenaline flowing in his body propelled him toward home in a time shorter than usual.

Upon arriving home, he greeted his mother who had been anxiously waiting for him. She looked at him with a sense of relief and said, "Boy, where have you been?"

With a smile on his face, he now removed the burlap sack from his shoulder and swung it around so that his mother could see the load of fish he had caught, as he said, "Look what I caught, Mom."

With a smile of satisfaction on her face, she said, "Give them to me, and I will get someone to help clean them. We will cook them tonight."

As much as David enjoyed fishing, the whip-poor-will now had begun to take center stage, one that influenced his entire family to begin a concerted effort in search of the whip-poor-will love song.

The last encounter with seeing a whip-poor-will that propelled Samuel's family, especially David, into a concerted effort in search of the whip-poor-will love song

After the momentous encounter with seeing the whip-poor-wills in their dancing and courting scheme, and after Samuel had experienced the unforgettable visionary dream with all its splendor and glorious images, it had become clear that this had left an unforgettable impression upon the entire family. It was an experience that would forever have an impact on their lives, one that would move them to learn more and more about the whip-poor-will and its love song.

Although Samuel, Anne, and David had the fortune of seeing a whip-poor-will once or twice more, as they could recall, the last one that stood out in their mind was when they saw a whip-poor-will indulging in a water puddle bath.

On this beautiful summer evening, Samuel, Anne, and this time along with David were sitting on the porch for the usual wind-down time. Only on this occasion, it was a Saturday evening, an evening that allowed them to stay up a little later than usual because the upcoming Sunday was a day when Samuel and his family would attend church. It was a day of worship and rest.

Samuel and Anne sat in their respective chairs on their front porch. David now had reached the age when he no longer sat on the steps below; rather, he now sat in a chair near his father and mother. The other siblings had already opted to go to their rooms or other favorite places inside the house to play their favorite games or have their own private conversations. Not so with David; for he most often enjoyed being around his parents and other older people to listen to them share their stories of their experiences that provided much wisdom for him.

On this beautiful summer day, a day in which rain had occurred earlier that morning, water was still present in some of the sunken holes in the dirt road near the garden.

Just before darkness had overtaken daylight, Samuel, Anne, and this time, along with David had another rare opportunity to see a glimpse of a whip-poor-will, this time, taking a water bath.

Suddenly, as they were quietly carrying on their casual conversation, they saw a movement of a bird making waves in one of the shallow water puddles near the garden. They could not tell whether it was a male or female whip-poor-will.

As they looked in the direction of the whip-poor-will making waves in the water puddle, they took care to remain still and quiet.

Over the years, they had learned that chickens and other birds often took water baths as a way to wash their bodies, helping to remove excess oil and possible parasites.

Shortly thereafter, the whip-poor-will disappeared into the darkness of the wooded area nearby. Again, it was noticed by David and his parents that about five minutes after the disappearance of the whip-poor-will which they saw, several whip-poor-wills began their usual singing in the night.

David was so excited, so much so that he could not hold his curiosity in. Now he was more determined than ever to find out more about the whip-poor-will and exactly what it is singing about. David asked his parents an all-important question: "What makes the whip-poor-will and its song so special to you?" It was a question that led to an ongoing dialogue.

CHAPTER 3

A Dialogue between Samuel, Anne, and David That Served as an Impetus for David to Take the Lead in Continuing the Journey in Search of the Whip-poor-will Love Song

By now, it was clear that David was the one chosen to begin taking the lead in learning more about the whip-poor-will song and the whip-poor-will in general. David was now in his junior year in high school.

On this occasion, it was one Sunday afternoon, a beautiful summer day, ideal for sitting on the porch. Samuel and his family had returned home from morning church service. Routinely, unless they decided to visit the sick or visit friends and family, they would sit on the front porch, depending on the weather.

On this beautiful Sunday afternoon, as the family often did, they all began by sitting on the porch together. However, the other children opted to go elsewhere; in the house, or get involved in other outdoor activities of their choosing. However, on this occasion, David would stay on the porch with his parents as he often did.

It was time for Samuel and Anne to begin their dialogue with David by explaining to him how the whip-poor-will and its song had influenced their love for one another and their family in general.

As usual, his father would begin the conversation. Only this time, it would be more like a dialogue, one in which each one,

Samuel, Anne, and David would give their individual input to the total discussion.

As Samuel began the conversation, it was clear that he and Anne wanted to center the dialogue between them in a way to share with David how the whip-poor-will and its song had inspired them, over the years, to grow stronger in their relationship with each other, as well as with their family in general.

SAMUEL: (*looking directly at David*) I may not know much from books about biology, science, and the study of birds, and what they tell me about living things, but I do know that over the years, I have learned much about practical biology, science, and the study of birds, and what they tell me about living things. I have been blessed in learning much about these subjects and much more through practical life experience.

DAVID: (*in responding to what his father said*) Daddy, I cannot count the many times you have reminded us that you only have a fourth-grade education. But here is what I have learned to know about you in a personal way. You may not have a lot of formal education. However, what you have shown me over the years is that you have a rich informal education. You are one of the smartest men I know. There is no doubt in my mind you could run circles around many who have a lot of formal education.

ANNE: (*looking directly at David*) As a former teacher, I was required to have some knowledge of book biology, science, and the study of birds, along with other general education, but still, my book knowledge does not rise to the level of practical knowledge that I have gained about these things through practical life experience. And by the way, David, you perhaps sometimes wonder how your father has grasped a solid knowledge of the English language over the years. One reason is that he volunteered me to teach him things such as understanding subject and verb agreement; the difference between present tense, past tense, and future tense; and using the dictionary to learn how to spell and define words to increase his vocabulary. And basic math, and so on. (*now looking at Samuel with an assuring smile*) If I were his teacher in school, I would have given him a high school diploma years ago.

DAVID: (*now looking directly at his mother*) Although you have always encouraged me to do my very best in school and continue my education, what impressed me the most about you as a mother is that you have shown us what it means to be a dedicated wife and mother for the whole family. You have stood by Daddy all the way. And you have stood by me and my brothers and sisters all the way. You have taught us what it means to love God and one another. Thank you, Mom. Thank you, Daddy. I am proud of you, Mom. Thank you, Daddy. I am so proud of you both. (*standing up and walking over to his mother to hug her*) I love you, and will always be proud of you and what you have done for our family. (*and likewise he walked over to his father and laid his hand on his shoulder*) Daddy, I love you and will always be proud of how both of you have shown us what it means to love God and one another.

Not willing to lose this momentum in this special dialogue with David, Samuel seized the moment to explain how the whip-poor-will had influenced his relationship with Anne and his family and what it really means to love God and one another.

Continuing the dialogue: How the whip-poor-will has influenced their relation with each other and family and what it really means to love one another

SAMUEL: (*leaned back in his chair and took a deep breath, pausing a moment, and then slowly inhaling the soft southern breeze filled with the sweet fragrance of roses and other yard flowers. His countenance now took on an expression of one meditating on beautiful thoughts as he said with a calming smile on his face*) David, your mother and I want to share with you how the whip-poor-will and its singing has influenced us over the years.

DAVID: (*upon hearing his father say this, David shuffled his body to the edge of his seat with great anticipation, as he said with a sense of solemnity in his voice*) I consider myself privileged and honored that you selected me to be the first to have you and Mom share your experience with me.

ANNE: (*now reminding David why she and Samuel wanted to share this information with him first*) David, your father and I have been so impressed over the years by observing how you love animals, birds, and the outdoors in general. And it did not go unnoticed that you often chose to sit on the steps of the porch and listen to us talk about things in life that did not necessarily interest young people. Even though your brothers and sisters most often chose to gravitate to things that are normally more exciting to young people, yet you most often opted to sit and talk with us.

DAVID: (*with an air of gratitude and respect in his voice*) Thank you, Mom and Daddy, for selecting me to receive this treasured information. Surely, this is a reminder that parents are paying attention to us, even when we, as young people, think they are not.

SAMUEL: (*now looking straight at David*) Your mother and I agreed to choose you to share this special information with you first because you are the one child in the family who has shown us, over the years, that you, too, have a special interest in outdoor life, especially the whip-poor-wills and their singing in the night.

It is our belief that God has revealed to us that He has chosen the whip-poor-will to convey a special message of love to us. Over the years, Anne and I have been inspired by the whip-poor-will and its singing in the night. Although we are aware that many believe it is singing its name, however, we believe it is being used by God in a special way to not only just sing about love but to also show us what real love means.

DAVID: (*as he was taking in what his father was saying, he looked at him, and then he focused his eyes on his mother*) Mother, how has the whip-poor-will influenced you and Daddy over the years? Was it because you believe that the whip-poor-will is singing about love? How did the whip-poor-will singing influence you and Daddy?

ANNE: (*with a sense of satisfaction on her face as a result of the all-important questions that David had asked, she now looked at him with a warm smile*) The whip-poor-will shows us that love is what love does.

SAMUEL: (*as Samuel was listening to David's questions and Anne's brief answer, he looked at David*) Think about all that we learned about love and its meaning in the many Sunday school classes and Bible study classes, in which we participated and the many sermons we heard. David, to begin answering your questions, first we need to look at what is love. And second, we need to look at what love does. In doing so, it will help you to see how the whip-poor-will love song has influenced us. Your mother and I will do our very best to share with you what we have learned about love. Let us begin by looking at what is love:

What is love?

As we attempt to define *what is love*, it is important for us to understand that, first and foremost, our definition must be informed by the Scriptures. Real love means much more than how it is described or used in the secular world. We all have our own intuitive understanding of love because love is an integral part of our human experience. Philosophers and theologians have debated the question: what is love? Thousands upon thousands of books have been written on the subject. Still, love is one of the most used, misused, misunderstood, and cherished words in human history. It has been used to describe a relationship, a feeling, a passion, an action, and more. To begin to understand what is love, we must look at what the Scriptures say about love.

What do the scriptures say about love?

Over the years, I, as a Sunday school teacher, have learned that the Scriptures use several different Hebrew and Greek words to describe the English word *love*. However, I will focus on the Greek word *Agapao* (love), which is defined as sacrificial, unconditional love, a love that seeks the best for others.

This is the type of love that God has for us. In fact, the very nature of God is love. Love is a core attribute of God's character (1 John 4:8, 16). He is the source of love. His unconditional love is offered to all to receive. This *Agapao* love is a divine gift from God. And those who receive it become channels through which it can flow. John 3:16 is a good example of this; for we are told that "God so loved the world that He gave His only begotten Son, that whoever believes in Him shall not perish but have everlasting life."

It is important to remember, however, that all humans, as part of God's creation, receive the ability to demonstrate that which we call common love, such as romantic love, affectionate love, and so on. However, common love is different from *Agapao* love in that it is limited by our human limitations and it needs to be reciprocated.

I could write volumes upon volumes of books about God's love, but the most important thing to remember is that the theme of love flows throughout the Holy Scriptures.

At this juncture, it is important to remember God's love is shown in all its creation. Remember, too, the whip-poor-will as part of God's creation has been given the innate ability to proclaim and demonstrate God's love in its own unique way, although we humans have failed to fully recognize this truth.

Remember, it is cited throughout the Scriptures in many ways that God speaks to us. In Psalm 19:2–3, we are told that God's speech is uttered day unto day and night unto night, and there is no speech or language where God's ordained voice is not heard. This is important to know if we are to understand that He is using the whip-poor-will to convey His message of love to us in its own unique language.

What love does

As Anne was listening to Samuel explain to David what love is, she was convinced that it was equally important for him to know what love does. She needed to explain to him that true love cannot be expressed in a static way. Rather, it must be expressed in a dynamic way.

ANNE: Love is action. God demonstrates His love for us in an active way. He loved us yesterday. He loves us today, and He will love us forever. Although I do not want to sound too *teachy*, I believe for one to understand what real love does, one must look at its main ingredients and some of their synonyms:

- *Commitment* means to promise, to pledge, and to vow.
- *Loyalty* means dependability, consistency, or steadfastness.
- *Giving* means granting, bestowing, and presenting.
- *Receiving* means accepting, collecting, and acquiring.
- *Faithfulness* means devotion, trustworthiness, and fidelity.
- *Honor* means to treat others with respect and to value.
- *Looking out for the well-being of the other person* (self-explanatory)

ANNE: Remember, these are the main ingredients that are found in real love. Also, it is important for me to emphasize that the nature of love is to give. However, for real love to flow, there must be giving and receiving. It has been said that real love must be like a bucket beneath a waterfall: it keeps on receiving, and it keeps on overflowing in its giving. Another way to describe dynamic love is that it is like an unbroken circle that goes around and around as long as the relationship is one of giving and receiving. In essence, it goes without saying each of these ingredients found in real love must be expressed or manifested in a dynamic way. The whip-poor-will's actions toward one another show us that what love does is a by-product of what love is.

Samuel and Anne explain how the whip-poor-wills' love shows them what love in action means

Samuel and Anne, as indicated earlier, had the rare opportunity to visually see a whip-poor-will only a few times over the span of nearly fifty years. However, over this same period of time, they had heard the whip-poor-will sing its song thousands upon thousands of times from early spring to late summer during the night.

Also, during these years, they had mentally cataloged the time period of the whip-poor-wills' migration, and how consistent they were in how they determined the circuits within which each group would habitat during the mating and nurturing season; one which always begins early spring and ends late summer of each year in southwestern Alabama.

After which, they would begin migrating to the Gulf Shores, to Central and South America. It had become clear that their pattern of migration was cyclical: each year they migrated from North America, to Central America, to South America, and returned from South America to Central America to North America.

Also, they had noticed how the phases of the moon played a very important part during the gestation periods and how it affected the young whip-poor-wills during their development and nurturing stages. In addition, they noticed how their pattern of migration is controlled by the seasons and climate in each region.

Over the years, Samuel and Anne not only had the wonderful opportunity to hear the whip-poor-will sing its song each night, from early spring to late summer each year; they also did personal research to learn more about the whip-poor-will bird and its breeding habits, nesting habits, feeding habits, and how the male and female shared in raising their little ones, and so on.

Documented research or written information about the whip-poor-will was very limited for Samuel and Anne and others who were born during the GI generation (1900–1924). And even today, this is true, although to a lesser degree.

Again, the question can be asked: Why is this so? The short answer, as indicated earlier, is that the whip-poor-will bird sleeps during the day and therefore is seen by less than 1 percent of the world's population although many have heard it sing during the night.

Although Samuel and Anne were among the fortunate few in the 1 percent club who had the rare opportunity to see a whip-poor-will, they never had the opportunity to visually track the whip-poor-will in all its actions during its habitation periods. Mostly, their observations about its habits and location were determined by listening to its singing at night.

This, in and of itself, convinced them that the whip-poor-will was singing an all-important love song to each other and to us, and it has a far-reaching message, one that shows what it means to love God and one another. They also were convinced that the whip-poor-will's consistent actions demonstrated the main ingredients of love.

And over the years, Samuel and Anne became more and more aware that the whip-poor-will love song, demonstrated by its faithful and consistent actions, had influenced and strengthened their love in their marriage and their family over the years. As years passed, they were convinced the whip-poor-will was singing a love song that was real. And the by-product was one that was proven by faithful and consistent action in all they did. All in all, they believed God was using the whip-poor-will to convey the message of love to us in a special way.

Additionally, they had heard the whip-poor-will sing up close enough to know that its song had three phrases in it. But what they had not learned at this point was just the wording of the three phrases used; one that could be translated into English. They knew they did not have the necessary analyzing tools to discover this in detail, but they had faith that David someday would.

David chosen to be the one to continue the search for the whip-poor-will love song and its meaning

They also knew that David would be the chosen one to continue searching for the answer to this song. They knew that he must be the one to learn more about the whip-poor-will and thereby increase his knowledge of the whip-poor-will and its love song.

Additionally, it was their hope that David would be encouraged to continue this search as he gained access to advanced technology that would increasingly evolve during his lifetime.

Samuel was now ready to pass on to David the catalog of information that he and Anne had compiled over the last fifty years, during which time they had been increasingly drawn to the whip-poor-will and its song. Now as part of their final charge, Samuel and Anne presented to David the catalog of information that they had carefully filed in the home safe-box with other important family records.

With final words of encouragement and with the confidence that their dialogue with David would catapult him into the leadership role in the search for the whip-poor-will love song, they hugged David as they said, "Deep down in our heart, we believe you will be successful in your endeavor."

Yet David had one final question: "What is the most important first step I should take in this endeavor?"

Samuel and Anne, in unison, said, "The bird is in your hand."

Samuel has a flashback of the visionary dream of seeing and hearing the whip-poor-wills courting and dance scene

The very night after Samuel and Anne had given David his final *marching orders*, Samuel was overcome with a flashback of the dream and vision he had before: He saw a picture of the whip-poor-wills courting and dancing in what appeared to be picture-perfect light. In the background, he saw beautiful mountainous streams of water cascading from the sky. In each direction he looked, he saw skies painted with rainbow colors that presented the most picturesque skies he had ever seen. Coupled with this was the symphonic sound of the sweetest music he had ever heard ringing from all around. And at the same time the whip-poor-wills were dancing, there also appeared angelic beings dancing and singing in the background to the beat of the music.

The song the angelic beings were singing did not appear to be the singing of the name "whip-poor-will." Rather, he heard words that included something about real love.

$\asymp$

CHAPTER 4

DAVID, THE REPRESENTATIVE OF THE TRADITIONALIST GENERATION (1925–1945) IS THRUST INTO THE FOREFRONT IN THE SEARCH FOR THE WHIP-POOR-WILL LOVE SONG

Now that "the bird was in David's hand," it was time for him to take the lead in searching for the whip-poor-will love song.

David's generation, 1925–1945, commonly called the Traditional Generation, in which he was born, like any other generation, must know that each generation is invariably responsible for its own call to learn from the past generation, its history, and the best of its values and traditions and carry the best of it into its current generation and subsequently pass it on to the next generation.

Each generation must remember it stands on the shoulders of the preceding generations. Each generation is responsible for *building bridges* for the next generation to cross over to the next.

Each generation is responsible for preserving the history of its preceding generations. It has been said that to improve, we must not allow ourselves to be anemic of the past. It also has been said, "Each generation must ask God to give it the courage to change the things that need to be changed and the serenity to accept the things that must not or cannot be changed and the wisdom to know the difference."

David, like each member of God's creation, has been given a special ministry to fulfill. As God has given the whip-poor-will a love song to deliver to each other and to us, He has given David a special call to capture the wording and meaning of the whip-poor-will's love song and pass it on to others, one which will have a positive influence on all who use its message wisely.

David endeavors to further prepare himself for the unique task of searching for the whip-poor-will love song

David was now sixty years old. His beloved parents, Samuel and Anne, had departed this life to their heavenly home where their rewards were sure. Although he would always miss them, he took comfort in knowing that their wonderful legacy and sweet memories would live on forever.

They had taught him well in words and deeds. They not only taught him what love is, but they also taught him what love does.

And he was keenly aware that he had been given the charge of searching for and finding the answer to the meaning of the whip-poor-will love song: What is it singing? And passing on his findings to his generation and generations to come.

As was indicated earlier, David had two older brothers and two older sisters. Each one had answered the call to their own individual ministry in life as they were led to do so. The oldest sister became a career teacher and housewife. The oldest brother, along with his wife, was successfully raising his family on the family farmland. He was the one designated to carry on the family business after their parents passed.

The second oldest sister attended college in another state where she and her husband were raising their family.

Remember: the Korean War took its toll on families in the early and mid-1950s. The second oldest son was drafted into the army and died in combat during the Korean War.

David himself was also drafted during the Korean War. After two years of service, he was honorably discharged and was able to use the GI Bill to attend college.

Because David always had a love for the outdoors and had a special interest in how things in all of God's creation grow and function within the general scheme of creation, it is no coincidence he chose to study biology and science. After four years of college, he received a double major in biology and general science education. While in college, he met Priscilla, who was from Long Island, New York. Soon after graduating from college, they became husband and wife.

It has been said, "Love will find a way." Well, the love of his life, his wife Priscilla, led him to Long Island, New York, where he taught biology education and general science in the public school system for thirty years. During this time, his wife was employed as a social worker in addition to fulfilling the role of wife and mother. They were blessed with one son, Jonathan.

David enjoyed teaching and living on Long Island and occasionally traveling to New York City, the Big Apple; however, in the back of his mind, he always knew he would someday go back to Alabama. It has been said, "You can take a boy out of the country, but you cannot take the country out of the boy." Although David could not recall ever hearing a whip-poor-will singing on Long Island, he never forgot the thousands upon thousands of times he heard them sing while growing up in Alabama.

And it goes without saying that he had never forgotten the charge that his father and mother gave him concerning the search for the whip-poor-will love song and the importance of passing on the message to others.

David is now ready to use his field of study, biology and general science, to begin an in-depth study of the whip-poor-will and its love song

With an ongoing desire to continue to learn more about the whip-poor-will and its love song, David was now ready to intensify his search to further organize the material that would help him discover more about the whip-poor-will and its love song. He believed one day he would be able to use this information to encourage others to take notice and appreciate how God is using the whip-poor-will and every member of His creation to proclaim His glory.

He suddenly realized that he needed to review the library of information about the whip-poor-will compiled by his parents, carefully stored in the boxes that had been given to him before he left home. He vividly remembered that he had carefully kept them safely locked up in a safe for future use. Now it was time to use them to continue to help compile as much information as possible in learning more about the whip-poor-will and its love song.

As David began reviewing the carefully detailed information that his parents had compiled on the whip-poor-will during their lifetime, he was amazed at the thoroughness of how they had organized their library of information. The more he read and examined his parents' library of information, the more he realized how valuable it would be because, by and large, their information was based on firsthand knowledge.

He was now, more than ever, ready to use his knowledge of biology and general science and his teaching experience to expand on what his parents had taught him. With this treasure of information as his resource, he was ready to expand his search to give the general public a broader view of how the whip-poor-will fit into the general scheme of God's creation and how it speaks to us today.

Yet at this juncture of searching for the whip-poor-will's love song, David knew that he needed to know more about the whip-poor-will in other aspects of its existence and the role it plays in God's creation. He concluded that he would use a topical approach in his endeavor without overwhelming the reader with too much scientific and technical information.

CHAPTER 5

THE WHIP-POOR-WILL: WHAT KIND OF BIRD IS IT

As indicated earlier, the whip-poor-will is near the bottom of the totem pole in terms of its popularity in America or worldwide in general. For example, we have already learned it is not listed as a state bird in all fifty states in America. Nor is it considered to be one of the most attractive birds in terms of how we measure beauty. Also, it is a bird that has presumably been seen by less than 1 percent of the world's population. Yet in many parts of America, especially in the rural areas, most everyone can recall hearing a whip-poor-will sing at night. Most have decided that it is singing its name.

However, David intends to show that it is singing a love song to each other and to us. Further, David intends to conclude his search with the help of his son, Jonathan, to translate the words of the whip-poor-will's love song into the English language. How exciting is this!

Toward this end, he knows he must seek to discover what kind of bird the whip-poor-will is. To accomplish this, David knows that he would need to gather information from those who specialize in studying birds, those who house birds in US zoos, and those who are *bird-watchers*. And even some like *angels unaware* who crossed David's path, most of whom remain anonymous, even to this day.

To facilitate this process, David and his family often traveled back to Alabama during his spring, easter, and summer breaks.

Within this process, he knew that he needed to focus on listening to the whip-poor-will sing at night and to talk with those who have lived in Alabama on a permanent basis, about the whip-poor-will and its singing. In this process, David was amazed at how much practical and nuanced information he was able to broach from Alabamians, bits and pieces of information that could not be obtained from general academia.

A rare interview and dialogue with Mr. Bill, the wise old man

David remembered his father once or twice had a talk with a man called Mr. Bill ("the Wise Old Man") living in southwestern Alabama. He is viewed as a mystery man who spends most of his time alone in the mountains of the Ararat (this is not the Mt. Ararat in Israel) region where he lives. The legend has it that no one really knows much about his background although it has been rumored that his ancestry goes all the way back to the Choctaw Indians.

He lives alone in a modest house near the bottom of one of the mountains in the Mt. Ararat region. Some have said he makes a daily trip up to one special mountain in the Mt. Ararat region. Some have asked him why he goes to this special mountain every day. He would simply tell them, "It is where I commune with my Creator and quietly blend in with the surrounding creation and listen to each part speak in its own language. Outdoors is where I find real-life peace and happiness. Up here in the mountains, I have learned to blend in with the birds and animals and the beauty of all God's surrounding creations. I can sit for hours just listening and watching the different birds sing their favored songs. The mockingbird is the most impressive during the daytime as it imitates the songs of dozens upon dozens of other birds. Its medley of songs can entertain you all day. However, the whip-poor-will is the star singer at night. It keeps me company at night with its night singing.

"I must have heard it sing its songs thousands of times from early spring to late August each year. I have learned that the whip-poor-wills are a lot like me in that they mostly stay to themselves and are very consistent in what they do. I am still trying to find out what they are singing. Just maybe someday I'll know."

Mr. Bill is rarely seen except when he makes occasional trips to the little town near the Tombigbee River to buy groceries or other items he might need.

Some of the older gentlemen always look forward to sitting in the courthouse yard on benches where old men sit, talking about pastimes or just bringing each other up to date on the latest rumored news in the community. However, one of their favorite pastimes gathering is to listen to Mr. Bill, the wise old man, share with them in storytelling time. No one else in town could come close to matching him during storytelling time. Mr. Bill had a way with words that exuded wisdom no one else could even come close to matching. He would spin his stories in a way that would leave the listeners spellbound. Upon finishing his stories, he would suddenly disappear from the crowd as if he were "an angel unaware."

David had heard his father mention that Mr. Bill and he met on several occasions, and their conversation usually centered around talking about birds, especially the whip-poor-will. This is the Mr. Bill that David is about to visit for a rare interview.

CHAPTER 6

The Interview with Mr. Bill,
the Wise Old Man

David, his wife Priscilla, and his son Jonathan met Mr. Bill, known as the wise old man in Southwest Alabama. After introducing himself and his family to Mr. Bill, David was confident that he had taken care of the salutatory protocol, and he was now ready to enter into an interview with Mr. Bill, the wise old man.

DAVID: Mr. Bill, I am so honored on this beautiful morning and so pleased to meet and talk with you today.

Mr. Bill gestured to David to step aside a few feet away from the others; after which he gently reminded him that he would feel more comfortable if he alone would interview him. David agreed, after which he took a few minutes to explain to his wife and his son Jonathan that Mr. Bill wanted to talk to him alone. The arrangement was accommodated. Priscilla and their son, Jonathan, and his fiancée agreed to return to Butler and wait for David to call them after the interview. David and Mr. Bill were now alone.

MR. BILL: I am mighty pleased to meet you. You don't look or talk like you're from around here. What neck of the woods are you from?

DAVID: (*Sensing that Mr. Bill might not be too open to a complete stranger, David made sure he let Mr. Bill know that he was just another Alabamian who would soon be coming back home*) I was born and raised right here in Choctaw County, Alabama. My father, Samuel, in his journal, mentioned that he and you talked with each other several times in the past and that the whip-poor-will bird was always at the center of the discussion. After being drafted into the army and serving during the Korean War, and after going to college, I later moved to Long Island, New York, where I and my family now lived. However, the country was still in my blood. I and my wife were planning on coming back to Alabama soon to live here in our retirement.

MR. BILL: (*After hearing David say he was born and raised in Alabama, and that his father had mentioned him in a journal he had kept, Mr. Bill's countenance on his face changed from a guarded expression to a more receptive expression*) We'll be mighty glad to see you come back home.

DAVID: (*sensing that Mr. Bill was more open to talking to a fellow Alabamian, David continued by asking Mr. Bill for permission to record his interview on tape*) I consider my interview with you to be very special. Is it okay if I record it?

MR. BILL: Yes, you have my permission.

DAVID: It is my understanding that you have lived in southwest Alabama nearly all your life.

MR. BILL: Yes, that's correct. Going on ninety years now, and I don't reckon I want to live anywhere else.

DAVID: I always thought Alabama is a wonderful place to live. I look forward to coming back home.

MR. BILL: I think you'll enjoy coming back and living here, especially if you like the outdoors like I do. You'll be able to once again enjoy fishing, hunting, and gardening or even bird-watching. For those of us who like outdoor life, there is always something to do year-round. Don't reckon I would trade it for anything in the world.

DAVID: I am looking forward to it.

MR. BILL: (*now noticing David as he adjusted his tape recorder to make sure it was working properly*). I hope your recorder is working okay.

DAVID: (*with an assuring smile on his face*) Yes, we're good to go.

BILL: (*recognizing the oral and the written traditions*) By the way, I have always been aware of how much information was lost over the years because it was mostly not passed on to the next generation. We did not have the ability to record or print information as you do. So you see, I was born when the oral tradition (by word of mouth) was the method we mostly used to pass on information. And because of this, we have lost a lot of our history, especially in individual families.

Immediately, in hearing Mr. Bill mention the oral tradition, David knew that he must acknowledge to him in a respectful way how much he appreciated how people in the oral tradition made the very best of communicating with one another and passing on information as well as they did.

DAVID: I am aware that during most of your early lifetime, there were little or no methods of recording information. Bookstores or libraries such as we have now were rare. Therefore, most information was passed on orally, resulting in people losing a lot of valuable information as well as history along the way.

Although I respect the oral tradition, yet I am aware it is important to receive information and put it in written or recorded form so that it can be passed on to those of us who are living in the written traditions and those living in generations and evolving traditions for years to come. This is the primary reason I want to record this interview with you. Surely, it will help the next generation benefit from your great storehouse of information. In other words, your legacy will live on for generations to come.

Sensing that David was sincere about what he was doing and that he wanted to pass on this information to others, he did not hesitate to encourage David to use his skills and teaching ability to pass on his knowledge to others.

MR. BILL: David, deep down inside, I really feel that God has brought you here for this interview and I want to do my part by sharing with you what little I know.

DAVID: I thank you for your encouragement. In my opinion, I believe God has uniquely prepared you with special wisdom about outdoor life. May I continue my questioning?

MR. BILL: Yes, you have my full attention.

DAVID: First, I want to call to your attention one thing that always stood out for me as I was growing up in Alabama. I always enjoyed listening to the whip-poor-will sing.

MR. BILL: (*Now the smile on his face changed from a subtle smile to a big satisfying smile as he heard David mention the whip-poor-will*). I must admit I love watching and listening to birds sing. However, the whip-poor-will bird stands out in my mind because it sings at night when most other animals and birds cease their usual noises. Each year, from early spring to late summer, you can hear them singing almost throughout the night with a loud pitch in their voice that can be heard miles away.

I have watched their habits over the years, how they work together, and how they look out for each other. It makes me think that if they sing to each other that long, it must be something about love.

DAVID: Most people who have heard them sing seem to think they are singing their name, whip-poor-will. What do you think?

Mr. Bill hinting that the whip-poor-will is singing about love

MR. BILL: (*now with a curious smile on his face*) Years ago I used to think they were singing their name. However, in the last forty years or so, I have come to think they are singing something else. It is my strong hunch they are singing about love. (*pausing for a moment, as being in deep thought*). And I often wondered if only the male whip-poor-will sings. But the more I think about it, I am led to believe both the male and female sing to one another. (*with a suggestive smile on his face*) Think about it, if they love each other, it makes sense that they both sing to each other as a way of communicating their messages as well as singing words of love. Wouldn't it be something special if we could come up with the words to their love song?

David now sensed Mr. Bill was onto something that would profoundly help him in his search for the whip-poor-will song. At this opportune time, he sensed a need to inquire further as to why Mr. Bill felt so strongly about both the male and female singing to each other. So David continued his questioning on this particular matter.

DAVID: Over the last forty years, have you gained additional information that influenced you to think you now hear them singing something other than their name?

MR. BILL: (*began massaging his hair as if to give himself more time to ponder the question David had asked*) Well, over the last forty years, other bird-watchers, especially some from down in Mobile, have told me what they have observed about the whip-poor-will's migration patterns. Most of them have confirmed what I have had occasion to notice about certain species, which I call different cousins of the whip-poor-will family. I am going to make my explanation simple by limiting my focus to two cousins: the eastern whip-poor-will and its first cousin, the chuck-will's-widow. This has a lot to do with what I think they are singing.

DAVID: This is very interesting that you are indicating there is more than one type or species of whip-poor-wills.

MR. BILL: Yes, this is what others have observed along with me in the last forty years. I and other bird-watchers in this area have learned this by observing how the two types of whip-poor-wills' migration patterns have changed during the last forty years.

DAVID: It is my understanding that you are referring to the eastern whip-poor-will and its first cousin, the chuck-will's-widow.

MR. BILL: Yes, I am. Furthermore, in my early childhood days, I discovered that the whip-poor-will was mistakenly identified with several other birds, as well.

DAVID: (*sensing that Mr. Bill was about to confirm what he had heard his father say about the whip-poor-will being mistakenly identified with other birds*) Was this later proven to be true, and why?

The whip-poor-will's migration pattern

MR. BILL: Yes, it was proven to be true, and I will explain why later, but first, I am going to focus on what I have learned about the whip-poor-wills' migration patterns in general. Their migration pattern is cyclical. Here is what I and others have noticed: During the winter, they migrate southward to Florida, to Central America, and to South America. And in early spring, they return from South America to Central America, and then to Florida, gradually migrating their way to this neck of the woods in southwest Alabama, arriving here about mid-March. It has been told to me that some of them, which I believe to be the eastern whip-poor-will, migrate as far as Canada in the summer. However, I am going to tell you what I know from my own personal observation of them in southwest Alabama in terms of their migration habits.

DAVID: (*now sensing that he needed clarification about the whip-poor-will's migration habits, he needed to ask a leading question*) Just what are their specific migration habits?

MR. BILL: I am getting to that point now. My fellow bird-watchers from the Mobile area and other parts of Alabama agree that the whip-poor-wills migrate about thirty-five miles each night. It is said the male whip-poor-wills come in about two weeks ahead of the females to stake out a designated place to determine the circuit in which each group is to settle. Once the females arrive, each one begins to pair off with a male partner and establish a nest in their predetermined circuit. Now the breeding preparation begins.

How do the whip-poor-wills build their nest

DAVID: How do the whip-poor-wills build their nests?

MR. BILL: Well, one thing is for sure: they are unlike other birds. They build their nests the same way each year. However, the way the whip-poor-wills build their nests differs from most other birds.

DAVID: (*sensing that he needed to know how their nests differ from other birds*) How does their nest differ from other birds?

MR. BILL: Although I have never seen a whip-poor-will in the act of building their nest, the rare occasion I had in finding a nest many years ago when I was younger, I discovered they do not build an actual nest. Other bird-watchers have confirmed what I saw. They agree with me that the whip-poor-wills do not build an actual nest. They simply build their makeshift nests on the ground among fallen leaves and other debris beneath low-branching trees, such as shrubbery pines, magnolia trees, sweetgum trees, and other trees and bushes with low limbs near the ground, which form a canopy around them, providing a shadow that shields them from daylight and providing a camouflaged setting that helps them blend in with the coloration of their surroundings, in addition to providing an ideal environment for sleeping during the daytime. The brown leaves, especially the oval-shaped magnolia leaves that are as much as five inches wide by seven inches long, make them ideal for the whip-poor-wills to hide themselves in. Yet within this setting, the nesting area is usually located near an open-field area that allows them to fly in the surrounding open space, usually just a few feet off the ground, feeding on insects.

At this juncture, David realized how Mr. Bill's observation about the whip-poor-will confirmed much of what his father had written about in his journal. He politely interrupted Mr. Bill's observation by saying in an encouraging way.

DAVID: Mr. Bill, I admire all the knowledge you have accumulated about the whip-poor-will over the years. I hope you do not mind me asking you all these questions.

MR. BILL: (*with a polite smile on his face*) I don't mind at all. In fact, it is pleasing to find someone your age who has a desire to learn from older people. So feel free to ask me any question about what little I have learned about the whip-poor-will.

DAVID: (*with this encouragement, David felt more at ease with continuing his questioning*) Help me to better understand how the whip-poor-wills breed, feed, and nurture their offspring.

It was clear that more and more Mr. Bill was sensing that David was placing a lot of value on what he had been saying about the whip-poor-will. Mr. Bill was now more open than ever to continue sharing what he had learned about the whip-poor-will, and more than ever he was now sensing that he needed to impress on David the importance of passing on knowledge to others. Although he knew that it might seem like an afterthought.

MR. BILL: David, I have always believed that God does not give us knowledge to be kept only for our self-benefit. Rather, He wants us to pass it on to others. I believe that God has brought us together for this very purpose. I am responsible for passing my information on to you orally, and I believe you understand that it is your responsibility to pass it on to others in writing.

DAVID: (*without any hesitation*) I am ready to continue the task ahead.

MR. BILL: Now back to your last question or request.

DAVID: Oh yes. Help me to understand how the whip-poor-wills breed, feed, and nurture their offspring.

How the whip-poor-wills breed, feed, and nurture their offspring

MR. BILL: It is necessary that I start by mentioning how the whip-poor-wills feed themselves.

How do whip-poor-wills feed themselves?

MR. BILL: First, I will start by mentioning how the whip-poor-will s feed themselves. To start, it is important to mention that they arrive in early spring—beginning in late March in this region. It is timed with when the insects start appearing on the scene. It is a reminder of how God provides food for all His creatures. The whip-poor-wills feed themselves by flying in open spaces, only a few feet off the ground. They catch flying insects beginning at dusk and into the night hours. They have a gaping wide mouth that some say can open up to two inches. They eat mainly mosquitoes, moths, and beetles including June beetles, gnats, dragonflies, and a host of other insects.

I have been told by many bird-watchers that the whip-poor-wills sometimes search out rotten logs and leaves for ants, caterpillars, beetles, and an assortment of worms, in addition to other insects. I have also talked to some of the more serious birds-watchers around here who have said that they have even found small birds, such as swamp sparrows, in their stomachs as a result of dissecting them. Although I, myself, have never witnessed this procedure.

DAVID: (*interjecting*) Oh, by the way, Mr. Bill, as a biology teacher, I have often used the dissection process on frogs, birds, and other animals, or insects as a teaching tool in my lab class. However, I have never dissected a whip-poor-will.

MR. BILL: I have heard this is one reason why future doctors are required to take biology classes. (*smilingly*) They practice operating on animals first. Oh yes, before I forget, there's something else I want to mention about the whip-poor-will.

DAVID: Please do tell me what it is.

MR. BILL: On several occasions, in the late evening just before dusk, I have had the privilege of seeing them drink water by flying low across a pond or other bodies of water, as they scoop it up into their gaping mouth. Sometimes we take for granted that water is necessary for living beings to survive.

DAVID: Mr. Bill, that is so true. It is interesting to note how often we forget that insects, for example, can be seen as a nuisance to us, but at the same time beneficial for whip-poor-wills, and other birds, and animals, in that they are food for the whip-poor-wills and other birds.

MR. BILL: Heck yes, especially down in this neck of the woods. It's comforting to know that the whip-poor-will and other birds and animals help curb the insect population. Think about the whip-poor-wills themselves. As told to me, they can eat thousands of mosquitoes and other flying insects in one night.

DAVID: It is a reminder that God, within the food cycle, indeed provides for all His creatures.

MR. BILL: I am reminded of an old song I heard someone sing years ago: The *big fish eat the little fish. The little fish eat the littler fish, and the littler fish eat the littlest fish…That's the way it goes, that's the way it goes, and that's how it's got to be.* Nevertheless, to stay on the subject, now I will tell you what I know or have heard about how the whip-poor-wills breed.

DAVID: Indeed, I would love to receive your input on this subject: how whip-poor-wills breed.

How do the whip-poor-wills breed

MR. BILL: Our next subject: How do the whip-poor-wills breed rightly follow the steps that we have already discussed: how do whip-poor-wills build their nest, and how do they feed? Think about it, maintaining their basic needs (obtaining food, etc.) to live on, first and foremost, is necessary for their survival.

DAVID: This is a reminder that birds and other creatures of nature are similar to humans in this respect, in that they first need their physiological needs (that is, their first basic need) met. This includes food, water, air, and even sleep.

MR. BILL: I thank you, David, for reminding me of this powerful truth. To be frank, I had never given this much thought. It's amazing how much we take things for granted. And of course, it makes sense that before they build a nest (home) for themselves and their offspring. They must first take care of themselves.

Now back to the question at hand. How do whip-poor-wills breed? Well, there are steps that must take place before they begin breeding.

Remember again, in their yearly migration patterns they begin their return trip from South America to Central America and arriving in Southwest Alabama from March through April of each year. My fellow bird-watchers from further south in the Mobile area, along with many in this area, agree that the whip-poor-wills migrate about thirty-five miles each night. It is said that the male whip-poor-wills come in about two weeks ahead of the females to stake out a designated place to determine the circuit in which each group is to settle. Once the females arrive, one begins to pair off with a male partner and build a nest within their predetermined circuit. Now the breeding preparation begins. I have never personally observed the whip-poor-wills' courting antics. However, by observing chickens and other birds mating, I am sure there are similarities in each group as to how they mate.

DAVID: Mr. Bill, I think your observation is right on key. Case in point, may I share with you what my father and mother witnessed what they saw during a rare observation of a male whip-poor-will and a female whip-poor-will courting and mating scheme.

MR. BILL: (*now filling with a childlike excitement*) I anxiously wait with bated breath.

David now realized that he had Mr. Bill's full attention. David repeated what his father and mother told him about what they observed during the whip-poor-wills courting and dancing scene as Mr. Bill listened attentively. Next, David told Mr. Bill about what his father had experienced in his visionary dream. It was a heavenly dream that he would never forget. David recited the dream from memory as told by his father.

Mr. Bill, who was also a genius in telling stories, was now spellbound by what David had told him in describing the visionary dream that David's father, Samuel, had witnessed.

MR. BILL: (*after being so captivated by the story David had told him*) Wow! David, it sounded so real. (*after catching his breath, he continued his input*) Although I have never seen whip-poor-wills in an actual mating scene, I have seen other birds go through their mating routines. I believe you and I can agree that the whip-poor-wills mating nuances are basically the same as other birds. In other words, birds will do what birds do.

DAVID: (*with an accommodating smile on his face*) Yes, I agree, birds will do what birds do.

MR. BILL: Obviously, this leads me to talk about the female laying her eggs in a designated nest. Years ago, when I was younger and had more curiosity and energy, and as a result of hearing the whip-poor-will singing in the same general location on several consecutive days, gave me an opportunity to discover a pattern: When you hear them singing in the same general location, it means that their nest is within the same area.

However, the incubating adults are incredibly well camouflaged by reason of the mottled color of their feathers that blend in with the leaves and other surrounding vegetation. This makes them almost impossible to locate unless you nearly step on them. Nevertheless, in my youthful days, I was determined to locate one of their nests. Early one morning, I ventured into the area where I had heard them singing the night before.

With a hoe in my hand, I carefully shuffled through the wooded area looking for one of their nests. Suddenly, I heard a rustling noise very close to where I was walking. I realized I had nearly stepped on a whip-poor-will nest as the adult bird began making a hissing and growling sound and at the same time fluttering her wings. After reaching a short distance from her nest, about ten feet, she continued fluttering her wings as if she were pretending to be injured. I did not attempt to do her any harm. Even as a youngster, I have always had respect for animals unless I am attacked by one. I quickly noticed there were two eggs in the nest. The white-cream-colored eggs were spotted with gray and brown colors. I was careful not to disturb the eggs in the nest. I was quite satisfied with just finding a whip-poor-will and her nest.

I was also very much aware that other predators, such as wild cats, certain species of snakes (rattlesnakes, cottonmouth/moccasins), or even wild animals are often prowling in the woods looking for food, including bird eggs. And it goes without saying that I never was too keen on walking in the woods, especially during the early spring and throughout the summer with all the thick grass, weeds, bramble briars, and other mixed vegetation constantly growing, which makes it difficult to see where you are walking.

DAVID: (*having heard Mr. Bill mention the word* snakes) Have you ever been bitten by a rattlesnake?

MR. BILL: No, but I have, on many occasions, seen rattlesnakes in this area. Most times I was able to see them at a safe distance. And as a result, I avoided them by walking away. On some occasions, I have been fortunate enough to hear the rattling sound rattlesnakes make. After that, I was taught to make two important decisions. (1) With a hoe in my hand, I knew that if I was at least ten feet from the snake, I could slowly move away. (2) Also, with a hoe in my hand, I knew that if I saw that the snake was within six feet from me, and making a rattling noise with its tail while in a coiled position, it could strike at any moment, if I made the wrong move, especially if I moved my feet. Hence, I learned to slowly raise my hoe in the air and make a sure chopping downward motion to its neck with all my might. Fortunately, my aim was accurate. On each occasion, the snake was killed, and I was safe. However, I have known others who were not as fortunate as I in that they were bitten by snakes. As a matter of fact, after having memories of the rattlesnake encounters, I lost interest in looking for another whip-poor-will nest. I was satisfied in knowing they were located within their designated circuit.

DAVID: Mr. Bill, I am glad that you were unharmed. Many scientists and snake experts list rattlesnakes, as well as some other snakes, as poisonous and can be deadly if they bite you. Also, it is said they can spew out a spray mist from their mouth that travels as far as six feet, which also contains poison. Pit vipers are commonly known as poisonous snakes.

MR. BILL: It was amazing that in my younger days, some who were bitten by rattlesnakes survived by using old folks' medical remedies. Oh, by the way, thanks for the scientific terms: *pit vipers*. I now have another term to add to my vocabulary.

David, in your studies and research, what are some of the names of predators of whip-poor-wills you have discovered?

List of names of predators of the whip-poor-wills that other bird-watchers and scientists have cited

DAVID: First, I will cite what my father and mother noted in their journal about the whip-poor-will predators. In reading my parents' journal, their list of predators included animals based on their firsthand experience, and from other bird-watchers, as well as from a few books they were able to find on this subject: foxes, raccoons, skunks, opossums, snakes, and stray cats, as well as wild cats.

MR. BILL: The list of whip-poor-wills' predators your parents gave you is close to what I would select. However, based on my conversations with other bird-watchers, and others who have lived in this area for many years, I will add coyotes to the list of predators. In fact, some in this area who raise a large flock of domestic chickens and turkeys indicated that coyotes often raid the chicken yards or turkey yards and drag them into the thick of the woods to eat them as part of their meat diet.

DAVID: Come to think of it, I heard my parents mention something about coyotes coming into barnyards at night, capturing domestic chickens and turkeys to be consumed as part of their meat diet.

MR. BILL: However, I want to mention more about snakes that we briefly talked about earlier. First of all, I must confess the topic of snakes has always aroused in me a special sense of fear, whether one is talking about a poisonous snake or a nonpoisonous snake, in part because I have had some personal encounters with snakes. It is one encounter I remember as if it happened just yesterday, although the incident happened years ago, during my youth. It was the day I was chased by a cottonmouth snake as I was walking near one of my favorite fishing holes in a creek located within walking distance from our family home. My mind was so focused on catching fish, one of my favorite pastimes, so much so that the thought of snakes was far from my mind. Suddenly, I heard a sound near the dirt road I was traveling along. As I turned around to see what it was, instantly, I saw a cottonmouth snake with its mouth wide open coming after me. Instinctively, I turned around and threw my fishing pole and bucket at it. As a result, it slowed the snake down, giving me time to run as fast as I could, or should I say, as fast as I had to. Needless to say, that ended my fishing trip on that particular day.

Oh, by the way, David, knowing that you grew up on a farm, and knowing that you studied and taught biology in school, would you share with me what you have learned about snakes?

DAVID: First of all, having been born and raised on a farm myself, I was always taught by my parents to be on the lookout for snakes, especially during the warm weather seasons, March through October. There were snakes in particular that I was told to be aware of because they are known to be poisonous: rattlesnakes, copperhead snakes, eastern coral snakes, and cottonmouth (also known as water moccasin) snakes. I recall my parents telling me that one of the best defenses against snakes is to "look where you are walking." In fact, this wise warning helped me from having a serious encounter with most snakes. However, the cottonmouth is more territorial-minded and aggressive than most other snakes. It did not take me long to discover this. And like you, fishing was one of my favorite pastime activities during my boyhood days. And, yes, I too recall being chased by a cottonmouth snake that ended my fishing trip on that day.

MR. BILL: (*with a big smile on his face*) After being chased by the cottonmouth snake, did it stop you from going fishing again?

DAVID: (*with a slight chuckle*) Heck no, but after my encounter with the cottonmouth chasing me, it taught me to always take my dogs with me for added protection.

Now back to your question asking me to share what I have learned about snakes as a result of studying and teaching biology. First of all, keeping in mind our talk about the predators of the whip-poor-wills, I think it is important to mention that most scientists indicate that many snakes are nocturnal, though not all. However, there are two important observations I need to reiterate:

1. Animals that are active at night and sleep during the day are known as nocturnal.

2. And animals that are active during the day and sleep at night are diurnal.

MR. BILL: (*with an accommodating smile on his face*) Thanks again, David, for adding two new words to my vocabulary: *nocturnal* and *diurnal*.

DAVID: You are welcome, Mr. Bill. It is important to know these words and their definitions to understand how this affects the safety of the whip-poor-wills. To further continue discussing this impact on the whip-poor-wills' safety, I want to mention that most scientists agree that snakes are neither entirely nocturnal nor entirely diurnal. This means that they can be active day or night. Also, we must keep in mind that snakes, in general, have a keen sense of smell.

MR. BILL: Wow! This is scary stuff. I did not know some snakes could be active at night. This means I have to add another layer of watchfulness at night.

DAVID: Yes, that is true. However, by knowing this, it helps us to be more alert, both day and night. Now in continuing our discussion, it is important to discuss other attributes of snakes that give them the ability to hunt at night. For instance, like most nocturnal animals, snakes, in general, have a keen sense of smell and hearing. In addition, snakes are cold-blooded animals and not warm-blooded like humans or some other animals. Therefore, some snakes can be active at night because they have the ability to detect infrared to see the heat signature of their prey. The point is that all parts of a snake's existence rely on external heat to operate, whether it is to feed, sense other predators, locate a partner, fight sickness and infection, or simply pump blood throughout its body. This helps to explain why they are not generally active through the winter months.

MR. BILL: David, one thing this conversation about snakes and other predators that threaten the survival of the whip-poor-wills is that the predators can hunt both day and night. And finally, before I forget, this snake conversation brings back the memory of my early boyhood days when my mother always had chickens and turkeys she kept in the barnyard at night. She would remind us that the chicken snakes would sometimes climb into the barnyards and catch chickens or even turkeys for food, or go into the chicken nests and eat the chicken eggs, or even baby chicks. I can still recall her mentioning for us to make sure we take a stick and poke around in the nest before sticking our hands in it. In fact, this is how the chicken snakes got their name, chicken snakes.

DAVID: Thanks, Mr. Bill. This bit of information reminds us we need to add the chicken snakes to the list of possible predators of the whip-poor-wills. Now for the next question I have for you: What have you observed about the whip-poor-wills' incubation period?

The whip-poor-wills' incubating period

MR. BILL: First of all, over the years I have noticed that most nesting occurs from May to June. This is perfect timing in that it aligns with the many insects increasingly appearing on the scene. It is a time when plenty of food is available for both the adult whip-poor-wills, as well as for their little chicks. Also, over the years, it has been my observation that the whip-poor-wills time their nesting so that their little chicks will hatch about ten days before the full moon. It is said that the whip-poor-wills' incubation period, the time the adult sits on the nest of eggs, ranges between nineteen and twenty-one days. This time period is generally agreed upon by most bird-watchers I talk with. And I might add that another observation I have made each year is that the whip-poor-wills' most active singing occurs during the incubation period. It is said that after they hatch, the length of time the chicks remain in their nest ranges from three to eight days. However, sometimes the chicks are moved because of predator traffic. It is important to mention also, the dual role that both the male and female adult whip-poor-wills play during this period. For example, I am told by other bird-watchers that both the male and female take turns sitting on the nest during the incubation periods, especially if the female goes off and starts a new clutch nearby, while the male remains in charge of the first nest.

DAVID: Mr. Bill, what you are telling me thus far is reminding me that the incubation period is more involved than one would think.

MR. BILL: That's true. And there is more to be said about what goes on during the incubation and nurturing period. Take for example, how do the female and male adults feed their little chicks?

How do the adult whip-poor-wills feed their little chicks?

MR. BILL: Most bird-watchers, especially those who have paid close attention to the whip-poor-wills, agree with me that both the male and female feed their little chicks after they are hatched. Remember we said earlier, birds will do what birds do. Here is what I have observed over many years in watching other birds that build their nests above ground in trees, man-made birdhouses, under barn sheds, etc. Take the bluebirds for example: They often build their nests in man-made birdhouses. I have had on many occasions watched both the male and female help each other build their nest with straw, leaves, dry grass, and tiny little twigs from tree limbs, or other suitable items. One of the closest upfront views I have had occasion to experience was by watching the male and female house wren build their bird nest on the outside of my house near a windowsill, next to an old house fan, protruding through a sealed window. What made this view so special to me is that it was less than twenty feet from my front porch where I often spend my early morning hours while sitting and meditating, and sipping my morning coffee before getting involved in my daily activities, and I often repeated this routine in the early evenings during my wind-down time, after eating supper. Also, as a result of noticing the bluebirds build their nest on many occasions, I was able to pick up a similar pattern the two birds had in building their nests:

1. Both male and female participated in building the nest.
2. As each one flew into the nest and deposited straw, grass, or other items they normally use in building their nest, it would fly from the nest, and within seconds, the second bird, although I could not tell which one was male or female, flew in and deposited its nest-building items.

Over the years, I have seen the same pattern occurring as they build their nest. Oh yes, one other thing I need to mention: it soon became clear to me that it was always a male and female combination that had paired off for that year. Of course, you and I by now are very much aware that the whip-poor-will nest is different from other birds in general in that its nest is made nestled among leaves, straw, grass, and the like, resting on the ground, yet the male and female help each other build it.

DAVID: Mr. Bill, I thank you for this important information. Clearly, this is not something we learn by just reading books. It is a reminder of the importance of having an upfront personal view with our own eyes. In other words, "hands-on experience."

As an afterthought, Mr. Bill suddenly realized he, again, needed to thank David for recording their dialogue with each other.

MR. BILL: Thanks for recording this for the purpose of passing it on to others. It really means a lot to me. Next, I will talk about how the whip-poor-will feeds its little chicks after they are hatched."

How do the whip-poor-wills feed their little chicks after they are hatched?

MR. BILL: We have already talked about how the whip-poor-wills feed, in that they feed almost exclusively on a variety of insects. The next question we need to ask is this: How do the adult whip-poor-wills feed their recently hatched chicks? Remember, we have already discussed that both the male and female whip-poor-wills help each other build the nest and help each other during the incubation process. In addition, most bird-watchers agree that both the male and female assist in feeding their little hatchlings regurgitated food (insects). The next question that needs answering is this: how does *regurgitated* food get regurgitated?

How does the regurgitated food get regurgitated?

MR. BILL: I am not a scientist, but I've been told by other more serious bird-watchers that whip-poor-wills, like other birds, including chickens, do not have teeth to chop and grind their food. Instead, they have what we call a gizzard that grinds and processes the food before it can be digested and made ready for regurgitation and routed throughout the complete digestive system.

DAVID: Mr. Bill, the information you have given me is right on target in terms of how the adults feed their hatchlings. However, as I have already indicated, I am a biology teacher. And so with your permission, I'd like to expand on what you have already said about regurgitation.

MR. BILL: Please do so, David. Remember, as I said earlier, when your book knowledge is combined with my *hands-on experience*, we both learn from each other. So feel free to share with me what you have learned.

DAVID: Thanks for your encouragement. Well, you have already mentioned the hatchlings are fed with regurgitated food. And also you mentioned that whip-poor-wills, like other birds, have gizzards. So first, allow me to share with you what I have learned about the gizzard and how it functions in the digestive process from a biology teacher's perspective. First of all, I want to share with you what my parents shared with me about the rare occasion they were able to observe a whip-poor-will one late evening scratching and pecking in their freshly plowed garden.

MR. BILL: Please do so, David. For I would love to hear what they witnessed.

DAVID: Here is what I remember them saying: At first, we thought it was simply looking for worms or bugs. However, they later discovered it was pecking and picking up tiny pieces of tiny stones and grit into their mouth and ingesting them into their body. Additionally, they reminded me this was what chickens and other birds do.

MR. BILL: David, this is very interesting. It reminds me of the many times I have seen chickens and birds do the same thing. In fact, I have seen it happen so many times, I never gave it a second thought. Nor did I ever try to fully understand the real process of how they digest their food. I just remembered that I saw what I saw and recorded it in my memory bank. I just assumed birds will always do what birds do because that is how God made them.

DAVID: As I share with you what I have learned by studying and teaching biology, I believe it will give us a clearer understanding of why the whip-poor-wills, and other birds, ingest tiny stones and grit into their body. I will share with you what I have learned in my study books on the subject of biology and what it says about gizzards. In addition, I will share with you what I have learned as a result of teaching biology classes which included conducting biological lab classes. And that which required my students to dissect chickens and other birds to study the anatomy of their body parts, including the parts of the digestive system. Here is what I have studied and learned about the role the gizzard plays within the digestive system. First, it is important to remember that birds, including the whip-poor-will, do not have teeth in their mouth to chew their food up. Here is where the function of the gizzard comes into play. Without getting too technical, the simplest way to describe how the food that a bird swallows gets digested is as follows:

1. The bird swallows the food.
2. The food travels through its esophagus to the crop.
3. From there, it enters the glandular stomach, also known as the proventriculus where it secretes mucus, hydrochloric acids, and other chemicals.
4. Next, the food mixed with these chemicals travels to the muscular stomach, also known as the gizzard.
5. The function of the gizzard comes into play as it begins to contract: It pulsates and mixes the accumulated tiny stones, grit, and food (primarily insects) by acting as a grinding mechanism.
6. Also, there is a back-and-forth force feeding between the two stomachs, grinding it, and increasing exposure to digestive enzymes. At this point, the food has reached a consistency that makes regurgitation possible.

MR. BILL: Thanks, David. You have not only taught me more big words but also have explained in a clear way how the adult birds feed their baby chicks. Also, it has reminded me how important it is to take advantage of what we can learn not only from books but hands-on experience. You have shown me that explaining how the whip-poor-will feeds their baby chicks reminds me that the process is more involved than we ordinarily think. Having said this, explain what you mean when you use the word *regurgitation*.

DAVID: Well, the word *regurgitate* simply means to bring (swallowed food) up again to the mouth. This leads us to how the adult whip-poor-wills feed their baby chicks after they are hatched.

The whip-poor-will initially feed its hatched chicks using regurgitated food

DAVID: First, let me mention that most biologists believe the regurgitated food comes from the glandular stomach, which is called the proventriculus. This gives the adult whip-poor-wills the ability to feed their baby chicks with regurgitated food. It is a normal weaning process for feeding their young chicks.

MR. BILL: This helps me to understand what I have seen over the years as I watched the adult birds feed their young chicks. For many years, I have been able to watch birds on numerous occasions as they feed their little chicks after they are hatched. Whether their nest was located in a man-made birdhouse or nestled in a nearby tree, I saw a consistent pattern in how they fed their young chicks after they had been hatched. The first three to four days, I saw both parents fly, one after the other, into the nest with nothing hanging from their mouths. However, each time one of them flew into the nest, I heard the little baby chicks chirping as each one was being fed. And to your point, this stage was the regurgitation feeding stage. After the fourth day, I noticed the parents flew into the nest with food hanging from their mouths to feed their little chicks. The one thing I always noticed was that one parent would fly into the nest and feed the little chicks and then fly out within seconds. Almost immediately another parent would fly in and feed the little baby chicks. This pattern goes on until the parents have finished feeding each little chick, until the next meal. In this process, I discovered both parents, male and female, fed their little chicks. One year, this was made clear to me. It was a year that I had the occasion to watch two wrens build their nest on a windowsill, next to an old window fan. It was located about twenty feet from my front porch where I often sat while meditating or sipping on a cup of coffee. In other words, I had a front-row seat. One could ask, how did I come to the conclusion that only the parents, one female and one male, feed their little ones? Well, I have learned over the years that only one female and one male share the same nest.

DAVID: Thanks for sharing with me this very important information. My question to you is this: do you think both the male and female take part in raising and training their little ones in every phase of the breeding and nurturing process?

MR. BILL: Yes. Over the years, I have witnessed both the male and female parents participate in the entire breeding and nurturing process.

DAVID: It makes sense that both parents participate in the entire process, doesn't it?

MR. BILL: Yes, it does. It's a reminder that both male and female whip-poor-will parents participate in every phase of raising their little ones up to and including the time the little ones are mature enough to fly away and live on their own. Oh yes, before I forget, you said something about how the birds (whip-poor-wills) feed their little chicks with regurgitated food. Do you remember I said I saw something hanging from the parent birds' mouths as they fed their little chicks? It makes sense. As you indicated, the feeding of their little chicks begins with regurgitated food but eventually graduates to feeding them more solid food.

DAVID: Yes, it makes sense that the parent birds begin feeding the little chicks with soft food (that which is regurgitated) and gradually begin feeding them with solid food as they mature during the weaning stages because during the first few days, the little baby chicks' digestive system is not able to handle solid food.

MR. BILL: Now that the little chicks have grown into the fledgling stage, we need to talk about the whip-poor-wills' migration patterns.

DAVID: Yes. This is very timely because we know that at this stage the young whip-poor-wills are at least sixty days old and are now ready to migrate with the adult birds.

How do the young whip-poor-wills factor into the migration patterns of the whip-poor-wills?

MR. BILL: Remember, I said earlier that in this part of the country, southwest Alabama, the whip-poor-wills arrive here in late March of each year and select their breeding locations. And from May to June, they produce one and sometimes two broods of baby chicks. After their hatching and nurturing stages are complete, as you have indicated earlier, the young whip-poor-wills are at least sixty days old and can fly and feed themselves. Therefore, they are ready to make the migratory journey. This makes sense because over the years, I, along with other bird-watchers, have discovered the whip-poor-wills begin migrating south, to Central America, and eventually to South America where they will remain for the winter. This means the adult whip-poor-wills migrate with their entire families. At this juncture, I need to reiterate what is said by many bird-watchers. The whip-poor-wills fly only at night, for about thirty-five miles before stopping to roost, feed, and rest. This pattern is continued until they reach their destination. And of course, they follow this same pattern as they return back to this area from South America to Central America, and finally back to southwest Alabama, late March to April, early spring.

DAVID: Thank you for sharing this very important bit of information. What is your observation about what has been indicated about the decrease in the population of whip-poor-wills over the years?

What is causing a decrease in the whip-poor-will population?

MR. BILL: According to my observation, as well as others I talk to, there has been a decrease in their population. Most of us around here make this claim based on the number of whip-poor-wills that we hear sing at night during the breeding season. Here are some reasons we folks around here think are causing a decrease in the whip-poor-will population:

1. There is less farming, especially small farming, in this part of the country.

2. There is more timber cutting and tree planting, causing less open fields. Remember: the whip-poor-wills like to make their nest on the edge of the woods, next to open fields.

3. Also, we have seen an increase in the number of gas or diesel-operated machinery over the years, resulting not only in more noise pollution but air pollution also.

4. The growth of our cities and their surrounding suburban areas have resulted in fewer trees, wild plants, and other natural habitats for animals and birds.

5. In addition, there has been an increase in the usage of insecticide and pesticide chemicals.

6. And lest I forget, I must also mention that we must remember whip-poor-wills often fly over roads or sit on roadways during their foraging for food during the early night, or even nights with a full moon. This makes them vulnerable to collisions with moving automobiles. These are the main reasons for the decline in their populations that are talked about around here.

DAVID: Many of these are some of the same observations that my father cited in his journal. The important point I want to make at this juncture is that my father and you, along with many others in southwest Alabama, have had the opportunity to observe the whip-poor-will migrations over many decades. This, in and of itself, contributes to the credibility of what you all have observed.

MR. BILL: That's true, after seeing or noticing something happening over a long period of time indeed gives more credibility to what is witnessed.

DAVID: Most of us, including scientists who have studied the whip-poor-will's behavior in recent years, indicate they migrate at night. However, I must highlight a very important point you made earlier about what you have heard other bird-watchers say: the whip-poor-wills migrate only at night and only fly about thirty-five miles for incremental stops. This means they stop over and roost and rest throughout the night and the following day. With this in mind, there is another dimension we must add: This also explains why the whip-poor-wills travel mostly overland to reach Central America, Mexico. This makes sense that they do not travel a long distance over water, due to their flying in increments of thirty-five miles. This further explains why during their migration they often have to fly over large cities in Georgia, parts of Florida, Alabama, Mississippi, Louisiana, and Texas, to avoid flying over the Gulf of Mexico. In recent years with the availability of GPS, some scientists who have begun using modern methods of tracking them have indicated the whip-poor-wills can be disoriented by the bright lights of cities. With this in mind, one can understand they are often attracted to the light and end up dying as a result of crashing into buildings, especially high-rise buildings. This could play a significant part in their population decrease. And I am sure that future research concerning the reason for their population decrease will be discovered through better tracking methods.

MR. BILL: (*with a smile on his face*) Combining your observation with mine indeed has made both of us more knowledgeable. This has been a good day. Next, let us talk about why the whip-poor-wills are mistakenly identified with other birds.

Why the whip-poor-wills are often mistakenly identified with other birds

MR. BILL: One reason this has so often happened is because, as we learned earlier, less than 1 percent of the world's population has visually seen a whip-poor-will. Although many have heard the whip-poor-will sing at night, some do not fully understand that they are nocturnal and therefore sleep during the day. And when they start moving about at dusk, as daylight is beginning to give way to darkness, and as one sees them flying only a few feet above the ground, catching insects for their daily food, one can only see a silhouette of what they look like. As a result, many who often see other birds with similar appearance mistakenly identify the whip-poor-will with other birds that can be seen or heard during the day.

DAVID: Your point is well taken. Over the years, based on your findings, what other birds have been mistakenly identified with the whip-poor-will?

MR. BILL: Well, I am sure you will agree with me that before we start making comparisons between the whip-poor-wills and other birds, we must first describe the whip-poor-will's physical appearance.

DAVID: Your point is well taken again. I look forward to hearing what you have to say about this.

MR. BILL: First of all, let's talk about what the whip-poor-will looks like in terms of shape, size, and their general appearance. Although I have never actually measured a whip-poor-will's size, nor have I had the opportunity to actually hold a live one in my hand. However, I have had occasions to look at one that had been killed as a result of it crashing into a moving vehicle. Come to think of it, I can still recall during my preteen years a fellow that lived in this neighborhood miraculously caught a whip-poor-will that was alive in one of his wire-trap cages. I was amazed at how similar they are to the common nighthawks in size and color of their feathers. I never did find out what happened to the whip-poor-will that was trapped. My guess is that it was released back into the wild habitat. David, being that you are a biology teacher, and have always had a strong interest in the whip-poor-will, I am sure you can shed more light on what they look like, in terms of their physical appearance.

DAVID: I thank you for asking me to share with you what I have learned about their physical appearance. Most scientists agree with me that a whip-poor-will, especially a chuck-will's-widow, which we have been focusing on, averages a weight of about six ounces. The average length is about twelve inches. The average wingspan is about twenty inches. They have a relatively large head and a short bill. They have a somewhat long tail rounded on the end. Their feet are weak, and their legs are short. This explains why they roost parallel on tree limbs. And this also explains why they usually hop about awkwardly on the ground. The color of their feathers is mottled with a mixture of reddish-brown feathers that are lined with black, brown, and white patterns. This mixture of colors allows them to easily blend in with their surroundings. Another important factor concerning whip-poor-wills is that they have been shown to have a tendency to live a solitary life and are not overly aggressive. In fact, most observers have discovered if an intruder gets too close to their nest, the parent may try to lead the intruder away by first flushing off the nest, flying a short distance and landing, feigning injury as they attempt to lead the potential threat away from the nest.

Mr. Bill: Thanks, David, for sharing with me this detailed information. I have heard others describe this information in bits and pieces. But you have done a good job of putting these pieces together to give us a more scientific study of the whip-poor-will. Now that you've given me a clearer idea of what a whip-poor-will looks like, it helps me to understand in what ways they are similar to other birds. There are three other birds that have been mistakenly identified with the whip-poor-will in my neck of the woods: the common nighthawk, the quail (also known as the bobwhite bird), and the mockingbird. Take, for instance, the common nighthawk. Why is the nighthawk sometimes misidentified with the whip-poor-will?

Why is the nighthawk sometimes misidentified with the whip-poor-will?

Mr. Bill: Prior to the 1900s, most people misidentified them with the whip-poor-will. Some still do so today, mainly because they are similar in appearance. They are similar in size and shape. Their feathers are cryptic in colors of reddish-brown, and black and gray mixture, which makes them difficult to spot within their surroundings. Their food mainly consists of insects as part of their daily diet. They tend to arrive in this area in early March and remain until late September. More serious bird-watchers around here say the common nighthawk, unlike the whip-poor-will, lays its eggs on bare ground in clearings, burned areas, or in small patches of sandy gravel, on bare rock or gravel. Incubation is mostly done by the female but is sometimes shared by the male, same as the whip-poor-will for about nineteen days. Both parents care for the young chicks, feeding them regurgitated insects, and eventually solid food. However, there are some differences in their behavior and hunting patterns. It is agreed by most bird-watchers in this area that the common nighthawk hunts food by day or night because they are not strictly nocturnal. And like the whip-poor-will, their main source of food is insects. I have, over the years, had the privilege of sighting them flying in late afternoons, and just before it gets too dark. On many occasions, I have heard them make a unique nasal sound during the late afternoon and occasionally into the night. In fact, their vocalization sound is one way of distinguishing them from the whip-poor-will. It is a nasal sound, peent. On several occasions while sitting on my front porch, I have seen the common nighthawk, especially in the late afternoon flying just above treetops. As a result, I have been able to visually see them flying high enough so that I could see the whitewing crossbars beneath each wing and noticed they have a forked tail. This is another way to distinguish them from a whip-poor-will. Also, I have had occasions to see them dive from high in the sky and make a boom-like sound with its wings as it pull from the dive. These are some of the behaviors that make them different from the whip-poor-will. However, because of their close similarity in body appearance, and their lust for insects, one can understand why they are sometimes misidentified with each other.

DAVID: Thanks for this very important information by citing first-hand experience over many years of being able to see the common nighthawk in action with your naked eye. Again, this, in and of itself, gives much credibility in helping us to understand the similarity and dissimilarity of the whip-poor-will and the common nighthawk.

MR. BILL: Well, I am sure you could add to what I said about the similarity and dissimilarity of the common nighthawk.

DAVID: We could talk about scientific findings in describing these two birds. However, in my opinion, what you shared with me is more than adequate for our discussion. To continue our discussion, what other birds are sometimes misidentified with the whip-poor-will?

The whip-poor-will has been misidentified with the bobwhite

MR. BILL: Well, in terms of physical appearance, another bird comes to mind, the bobwhite, a bird that we in this part of the country also call a quail. In this part of the country, quail is a popular game bird that is often hunted. Although I have never hunted a quail myself, some of my neighbors in this area have given us some quail meat. I must confess, quail meat is very tasty. In fact, down through the years, the Choctaw Indians who inhabited this part of the country considered the quail bird one of their favorite game meats. It was rumored that they had some way of catching them in specially made nets, although I was never able to get the full story on this. (*after realizing he was somewhat detouring away from the subject at hand*) Now back to our subject at hand.

DAVID: (*with an accommodating smile on his face*) I appreciate you giving me this very valuable input. For it is very important we remember to value our history.

MR. BILL: Thanks for your encouraging compliment. The main reason the bobwhites (quail) are often misidentified with the whip-poor-will is primarily because they are similar in feather coloration and somewhat similar in size, although the bob-whites are generally larger. The bobwhite gets its name from the characteristic whistling call, "bobwhite." It has a chunky, rounded-shaped body. Its feet are larger, and its legs longer, in comparison to the whip-poor-will. This allows them to run on the ground faster and fly higher and faster than a whip-poor-will. The bobwhite can be found year-round in grassland, open woodland areas, agricultural fields, roadsides, and wood edges. I have seen them feed throughout the day. Their diet consists of plants, grass seeds, wild berries, partridge peas, cultivated grains, ticks, snails, and grasshoppers. Of course, I am sure that others can add to this list. As you can see, their diet is different from the whip-poor-will. I recall on one occasion I saw two bobwhites, probably a male and a female, cross the yard not more than ten feet from where I was sitting on the porch. On many other occasions, I have seen them after having been flushed out of a grassland area, fly away in flocks. Oh, by the way, this is how hunters are able to shoot them from the air with their shotguns. Sometimes able to kill two or more with one shot. However, the question still remains as to why the whip-poor-will is sometimes misidentified with the bobwhite. The short answer is that the bobwhite is active during the daylight hours and therefore is seen more often, whereas the whip-poor-will is active at night, from dusk to dawn, and therefore has been seen by less than 1 percent of the world's population. The point is that one can understand that since they have similar feather coloration and are somewhat similar in size, they can be assumed to be whip-poor-wills, especially when many do not know that the whip-poor-will sleeps during the day.

DAVID: Thanks, Mr. Bill, for using your personal experience in explaining the difference between the bobwhite and the whip-poor-will. And in the process explain why you think the whip-poor-will is sometimes misidentified with the bobwhite. Listening to you talk about the bobwhite brought back memories of my father mentioning that he went bobwhite (quail) hunting a few times. Although I have never gone quail hunting, I can recall my father bringing quail meat home. And my mother had a way of cooking them in a way that made them one of the most tasty meats I have ever eaten. Again I thank you for helping me to refresh my wonderful memories of the bobwhite (quail) and why they are sometimes misidentified with the whip-poor-will.

CHAPTER 7

An Interlude: Mr. Bill Talks about the Encounter the Male and Female House Wrens Had with His Pet Cat

MR. BILL: It was early April. Spring was now in our midst. The insects were becoming more plentiful day by day. The wren birds, as well as other birds, knew that the multitude of insects, including the mosquitoes, were a needed source of their daily diet. This bit of information gave me more of a reason to appreciate birds, including the whip-poor-will, that feed on mosquitoes, for they help control the insect population. Also, I knew that beginning in April, insects such as mosquitoes were daily becoming a nuisance to humans and many animals. It is not just the biting and skin irritation they cause but also the bothersome humming noise they make as they seek to find a perfect spot to bite. I have been told by an old medical doctor that the female mosquito needs blood which contains proteins and iron to produce eggs. It was a reminder that my blood was a potential part of the mosquito's food chain. In addition, other bird-watchers have told me that scientists have said that they can also spread diseases such as malaria. Yet even with this awareness, this has never stopped me from regularly sitting on my front porch parts of the morning and evening hours, drinking coffee, ice-cold sweet tea, or just plain ice water. Also, in this neck of the woods, I have learned how to make various concoctions of home remedies such as mixtures of garlic juice, vinegar juice, and aloe vera juice to rub on our skin as a mosquito repellent.

DAVID: (*asking with an inquisitive look on his face*) I do not mean to interrupt you, but where do the wrens fit into this picture of misidentification?

MR. BILL: (*saying with an apologetic smile on his face*) Oh yes, I want to do this by, first of all, talking about the encounter a male and female wren had with my pet cat. Around this neck of the woods, we often call wrens *house-wrens* because they have a tendency to build their nest beneath porch ceilings, beneath roof eaves, or other places outside people's houses and other buildings with openings that provide a safe place for shelter from rain, and also serve as protection from predators. Case in point, early one April morning, as I sat on my porch, I noticed two parent wrens, I assumed to be male and female, begin building their nest in an opening next to an old window fan, located under the eaves of my house roof. The window fan had a small space between it and the window frame with its bottom resting on the eave, about seven feet above the ground level. It was located approximately fourteen feet from my porch. It gave me an eye-level view of the nest. I said to myself, this is a perfect place for a bird nest, and likewise, this will give me a close-up view to observe how wrens build their nest, how they incubate their eggs, how they feed their chicks right after they hatch, and how they nurture them until they are ready to fly on their own. Without a doubt, I had a front-row seat for watching wrens in their life activities.

Watching the wrens build their nest

MR. BILL: I was able to watch them fly in with straw, grass, small tree limb twigs, and other selected items in their mouths as they began building their nest not more than fourteen feet from my front porch. During the days I watched them build their nest, I was able to discover a pattern: it appeared that two wrens were involved in building the nest. I made what I think was a logical conclusion: it was one female and one male involved in the building process. The whole nest-building process takes about one week, six to seven days.

Observing the house wrens during the incubation period

Mr. Bill: There was a lull of activities after the nest-building was complete. The activities slowed down with only one adult guarding the nest. It is said the incubation period lasts about two weeks, fourteen days. During the incubation period, I noticed what appeared to be a male serving as a protector or watch guard during the incubation. Although it did not make much noise with me nearby, however, whenever my pet cat came on the porch where I often sit, the male wren would fly into the nearest tree or even from the edge of the eaves near the nest and begin to make a frantic-fussing noise. Clearly, it was a way of enticing the cat to leave the area. During the incubation period, the female leaves the nest from time to time to feed herself. At other times, it appeared the male was bringing food to feed the female adult while she sat on the eggs. After about two weeks, the little hatchlings arrived on the scene. Both adults, male and female, began feeding them in the nest.

Observing the wrens during the nurturing and feeding of their young chicks

Mr. Bill: The initial feeding is done by the regurgitation process which involves both the female and male adults, which lasts from three to four days. During this period of time, I was privileged to notice that one adult would fly in and feed their little chicks regurgitated food and immediately fly out, and within seconds another adult would fly in and do likewise. Again, my logical conclusion was that it was both adults, male and female, involved in the feeding process. Also, during this stage of feeding, both male and female become more watchful for potential predators, resulting in them making increased frantic noises from various locations near the nest, for they were instinctively aware that other animals with their strong sense of smell were causing them to begin making their way to the wrens' nest. Their ultimate goal, sad but true, is to feed on nest eggs and young chicks. It was now about three or four days after the little hatchlings had come on the scene. I noticed that my pet cat seemed to be taking special notice of the wrens' nest, as he began prowling near it from the edges of the roof eaves, or from a tree limb. In my mind's reasoning, I had trusted that my pet cat would never bother nor even have thought of entering the nest and eating the little baby chicks.

It never crossed my mind that animals, for the most part, do not reason on the same level as humans. Rather, they operate primarily on instinct. Suddenly, I had a scary thought: *What if my pet cat would let his desire for a tasty little baby chick override the domestic training I had given him? What if somehow he would be able to leap a short distance through the air and somehow reach the nest and eat the innocent little baby chicks?* Think about it, it was the first three or four days after their hatchings that I could hear them making tiny little chirpings, calling for food. And as a result, the adult wren would fly in and feed them. At this point, I, now, had become so attached to the little baby chicks and even the adult wrens, so much so, as if they were part of my family. Also, I had convinced myself that my pet cat had the same sentiment. However, I became uneasy when I saw my cat wander away from the porch from where we were sitting and began paying close attention to the nest and its surroundings.

After spending my routine early morning meditating while sitting on the front porch along with my pet cat, it was time for me to go inside, finish my breakfast, and prepare for my daily activities. As usual, I left my pet cat alone on the porch to venture on his own everyday activities such as catching lizards, and sometimes chipmunks, and the like. Now evening had arrived as my daily activities outdoors had been completed. Supper had been eaten. Again it was time for me to sit on my front porch and go into my usual *wind-down* time, which included drinking my last cup of coffee for the day. My pet cat came on the porch and sat in its usual spot. On this evening, both adult birds were making unusual frantic noises as they were jumping from tree limb to the roof eaves above the wrens' nest, while at the same time, neither one attempted to enter the nest. And then I looked at my pet cat, I noticed something different about him this time. His stomach looked fuller than usual. And he was licking his paws and making sweeping strokes across his mouth, alternating with its right-hand and left-hand paws. I said to myself, *This is what cats do after they have eaten.* After finishing my *wind-down time*, I entered my house, leaving my pet cat outside to spend the night in his specially built house on the outside because I had a policy of not allowing my pets to sleep inside my house. For in our neck of the woods, we always felt the cats and dogs had a sense of having more freedom when allowed to live in their natural habitat, outdoors. After all, they are nocturnal animals too.

Throughout the night, I could not get the adult wrens and their little chicks off my mind. Think about it, I had observed them preparing their nest and taking care of their little chicks for nearly a whole month so much so that I had grown attached to them as if they were part of my extended family. Two con-flicting thoughts kept entering my mind: *What if my pet cat felt the same way I did? Or did he allow his cat instinct to overcome him and lead him to enter into the wrens' nest and eat the little chicks?* Needless to say, I slept very little that night. I awoke the next morning and prepared my breakfast. After finishing eat-ing breakfast, I sat on the front porch sipping on my morning coffee. It was unusually quiet around the bird nest. The adult wrens could not be heard or seen entering or leaving the bird house, nor could I hear the sounds of their hungry little baby chicks chirping for food. Suddenly, an eerie feeling came over me. Yet I clung to the hope that all was well with my adopted wrens. After sitting on the porch for a while longer and medi-tating and pondering over the two conflicting thoughts I had earlier, I chose to look on the bright side: everything is alright with my little tiny feathered friends. Shortly thereafter I ended my morning routine on my porch and prepared for my daily activities, hoping everything was alright.

Now two days have passed. Still no sight or sound of my adopted adult wrens, nor their little baby chicks. Finally, I could not stand the agonizing feeling any longer. I said to myself, *It is only one way for you to find out what happened to your furry-feathered friends*. I located a ladder, placed it near the wrens' nest, and peeped inside. As I peeped inside, I saw what I did not want to accept before. On the inside of the nest, I saw cracked eggshells and a few pieces of the little baby chicks' tiny-ruffled feathers. It was a sad day for me. I tried to comfort myself by saying, "Just shut it out of your mind and go on with your daily activities." Well, it did not work, the more I tried, the more I was overcome with grief. After all these little feathered friends had become part of my family. Finally, I could not hold back my tears any longer. I sat alone and cried like a baby.

DAVID: (*saying with tears in his eyes, as he gave Mr. Bill a sympathetic look*) Your story was so touching. I do hope that all is well with you now.

MR. BILL: Thank you, David, for your kindness. I will get over it. It is not the first time. You see I have been around animals all my life, and I have a tendency to get too attached to my pets. Oh yes, my pet cat. There is another part of this story I had to deal with.

DAVID: What part was this?

MR. BILL: I had to accept the fact that my pet cat, although he was domesticated by me and clearly had a special attachment to me, was still a cat, and he had eaten the wrens' little baby chicks. At first, I had conflicting thoughts: Initially, I became angry with him so much so that I thought about punishing him by taking him far away from my house, hoping to never see him again. And as I pondered on this thought, suddenly a *better angel* in me reminded me that cats and other animals are created by God to participate in the food chain. Thanks to the better angel within me, it helped me to accept the fact that God has given animals a special type of innate instinct to hunt for food. It is a reality we must accept. And bird meat is one of cats' special foods. Well, to make a long story short, my pet cat is still with me, and we are still friends.

DAVID: Mr. Bill, you mention the food chain. I think sometimes we forget God has created all his creatures to be part of a food chain, either directly or indirectly. And by the way, Mr. Bill, I want to thank you for that touching story. Although you did not mention that the wren has ever been misidentified with the whip-poor-will. However, your story pointed out many behavior patterns of the wren that are similar to that of the whip-poor-will. Again, thank you for this valuable information.

CHAPTER 8

CONTINUING THE INTERVIEW WITH MR. BILL, THE WISE OLD MAN WHY THE MOCKINGBIRD IS SOMETIMES MISIDENTIFIED WITH THE WHIP-POOR-WILL

MR. BILL: You are welcome. Lest I forget, I have one more bird that I want to talk about and why it is the one bird that has caused people to think the whip-poor-will sings throughout the daytime. It is the mockingbird. First of all, the one thing that fascinates me about the mockingbird is its ability to mimic other birds, and even other animals, in its medley of songs. Some of the more serious bird-watchers have indicated that the mockingbird can learn as many as two hundred songs, mimicking sounds from their environment, including other birds, car alarms, and even creaky gates.

During my lifetime, I have had the privilege of watching and hearing them sing for hours while sitting on my front porch or sometimes beneath an oak tree. It is a special treat to hear them singing from a nearby tree or perched on a nearby fence wire. Sometimes they sing for hours without stopping, especially during their nesting seasons. By and large, they are friendly to humans unless one gets too close to their nest.

They are very territorial and protective of their designated areas. I have seen them dive down and peck a cat venturing too close to their territory and have even seen them chasing a crow in midair. Other bird-watchers in this area have indicated that some migrate a short distance southward in the winter. While others agree with me that some remain here year-round, considering their diets, one can understand why. Their year-round diet consists heavily of insects, worms, and even lizards but also fruits and berries. However, during the winter, their diet is mainly berries (wild and cultivated) and fruits (wild and cultivated).

DAVID: Again, I thank you, Mr. Bill, for giving me information that only hands-on experience can provide with authenticity. And you mentioned to me that their diet during the winter includes berries, fruits, and the like, explaining why, unlike the whip-poor-wills, they can live around here during the winter. You also mentioned that they can be heard singing throughout the day and sometimes parts of the night. Again, only hands-on experience can provide this type of information.

MR. BILL: Good observation, but finally, I want to say something important about a particular song I have heard them sing during the day. Please note I discovered this key information by listening to the mockingbirds sing throughout the day while sitting quietly on my front porch for hours at a time.

DAVID: (*with excitement in his voice*) I heard you say *key information.*' I'm anxiously waiting to hear what it is.

MR. BILL: (*with a smile on his face, Mr. Bill knew that he had evoked special curiosity in David*) Be patient, David. I plan to tell you just what it is. (*After a slight pause, Mr. Bill began explaining what he had discovered*) The one thing I had come to realize is that I had to sit still for a long period and pay close attention to every utterance the mockingbird was making. It was only then that I was able to hear the mockingbird sing the whip-poor-will's song. It happens so quickly, so much so, and if you do not pay close attention, you can miss what it is singing. You see, I have heard the whip-poor-will sing its songs close up, thousands upon thousands of times. And I am convinced that the whip-poor-will is singing something about love. The mockingbird was clearly trying to imitate the whip-poor-will's love song but could not exactly duplicate it.

And finally, let me say again, that the whip-poor-will is nocturnal and sleeps at night. Yet those who are fortunate enough to hear the mockingbird imitate the whip-poor-will song during the day assumed that it was the whip-poor-will itself. This is why some incorrectly misidentify the whip-poor-will with the mockingbird.

DAVID: (*with a look of exhilaration on his face*) Wow, Mr. Bill! This has been a good day. How can I express my gratitude to you for all the wonderful and very valuable information you have shared with me, stemming from what you have personally seen and heard over the many years of your life? I want you to know that the vast amount of things you have shared with me about the whip-poor-will and other birds will never be forgotten. Certainly, it is more authentic than any information I could have ever gotten by simply reading books on this subject. Also, it confirms a lot of what my parents recorded in their journal about birds and animals.

MR. BILL: David, it has been a pleasure sharing with you what I have had the privilege of witnessing over the many years. May we never forget that God has brought the two of us together for such a time as this, to observe and dialogue with one another about what each one of us has learned about birds, animals, and other aspects of God's creation. It was uplifting to see how each of us grew in knowledge of God's creation as we shared with each other: my personal hands-on experience with you, and your book-learning and real-life experience with me. Surely, as a result of our two experiences meshing together, it has evoked in us a humbling reminder: When people come together and share with one another, great things can happen.

I am confident that you are dedicated to using this information to pass it on to others in a way that will help people appreciate the world around us and understand how God uses every component, every member of His creation to declare His glory, each in its own unique way. And you have taken a particular interest in using the whip-poor-will and its song as one important example.

DAVID: (*glancing at his watch and realizing that he and Mr. Bill had talked for over three hours*) Mr. Bill, I want you to know I will always treasure this special interview with you. And I will always treasure the special storehouse of information you have provided me today.

MR. BILL: Likewise, and I thank you for your input. It is a reminder that we never get too old to learn.

DAVID: (*picking up his phone*) Please excuse me as I remind my wife and son, and his fiancée, who is in town, that I have completed my formal interview with you. I will tell them they can return to your house to pick me up. And while they are returning, it will give both of us a chance to talk "off the record," so to speak. (*having said this, he now turned off the tape recorder*)

MR. BILL: Please do. Meanwhile, we can just talk casually until your wife and son arrive.

DAVID: (*seizing the moment by sharing with Mr. Bill the beautiful memories he had of growing up on a farm. He talked of why he never felt alone on the farm*) There were many reasons I never felt alone on the family farm. First of all, it was on the farm where I learned that farming is essentially a twenty-four-hour, seven-days-a-week job. Even after one has worked from sunup to sundown, down on the farm, one is always on standby.

Another reason I never felt alone in Alabama is because I was raised in a large family and therefore always had someone to communicate and relate to. Also, on our farm, we raised a wide variety of animals that not only kept us busy but also kept us company in their own way. In addition, rarely a day went by without being able to see wild animals making their frequent appearances. And most of all, my favorite pastime was observing and listening to the numerous birds flying and singing around us.

Of course, as you have discovered by now, the whip-poor-will has always been one of my most favorite and mysterious birds because of their unique singing at night. Come to think of it, I never really had the experience of living alone during all the years growing up in Alabama. Mr. Bill, you have indicated to me that you have lived alone for many years. This leads me to a question about being alone: Do you ever feel like you are all alone, all by yourself with no one to relate to?

Mr. Bill explains to David why he never feels alone

MR. BILL: (*pondering the question David had asked him, Mr. Bill lifted his hand to his chin and began slowly rubbing it*) Over the years, I have learned that being alone from other people does not mean I am alone. Although I must confess that there are times when I miss being around other people, I have come to realize that not being around other people does not mean that I am alone.

To put this in the right perspective, I am reminded of what a preacher said in church. We were created by God, who is a Spirit. He is present everywhere at the same time. And He reminds us that He will never leave those who believe in Him alone. I am a Christian, and I believe in Him.

DAVID: I can attest to that, for I am a Christian also. And I am reminded of what God says in Psalm 19:1: "The heavens declare His glory." It is a reminder that all the mighty works of God's creation, each component of God's creation, in its own unique way, each in its own language, each in its own song, proclaims the glory of God. However, in our current hustle-and-bustle society, we are rarely able to get alone and be still and know that God is God, by hearing Him speak to us through every component, every aspect of His creation.

MR. BILL: Thanks for reminding me that you are a Christian. I commend your parents for giving you a well-rounded experience, book learning, biblical learning, and the ability to relate to God, others, and every aspect of His creation. You have helped me to further understand why I do not have to feel like I am alone.

Mr. Bill further explains why he never feels alone

MR. BILL: It is strange but true that one reason I never feel alone up here in the Mount Ararat region is because of what one of my old distant cousins told me a long time ago. He reminded me that his people were part of the Choctaw Indian tribe who used to live in the Mount Ararat region. I recall him saying it was an ideal location because it was near the Tombigbee River. And the Mount Ararat region nearby, with one of its tallest mountains reaching about six hundred feet above sea level, was ideal for many reasons:

1. It meant that we had protection against an enemy surprise attack because we were sitting "high and looking low," so to speak.
2. Living up in the mountains prevented them from being flooded out when heavy rains came.
3. Because we lived near the river, fishing and hunting were ideal, and many wild animals, and birds kept us company both day and night.
4. We could use our canoes to travel miles up and down the Tombigbee River. There was always something to do. My old distant cousin said he never felt alone.

Here I am now, living in the same region. Living up here in the mountains, a short distance from the Tombigbee River, I have the same feeling—that I am not alone. Think about it, I've got chickens in my yard, goats and a few cattle in the pasture, a vegetable garden to tend, and three cats and two dogs. All these I consider to be my extended family. And by the way, each has a way of speaking and relating to me, each in its own language.

Not only this, when I go up near the mountaintop, I discover that God meets me there. He walks and talks with me. He whispers in my ear and tells me I am His own. He tells me I am not alone, and the joy we share as we tarry there is like no other has ever known.

Not only this, as I walk through the forest and see the magnolia trees, the longleaf pines, the sweet gum trees, the oak trees, and many other unnamed trees, and hordes of beautiful flowers emanating their unique fragrance as I pass by, each speaks to me through the soft southern breeze. Each one speaks to me in its own language, reminding me I am not alone.

And then too throughout the day, I see the beautiful birds flying to and fro, and often landing on a nearby tree limb or a convenient fence wire, singing songs that bring sweet music to my ear, each one in its own language, each one with its own song, reminding me they are always near.

Not only this, I am tending my garden of vegetables and flowers, which gives off a sweet fragrance that penetrates my nostrils and awakens my sense of smell, while quietly telling me, each one with a language of its own, that God loves me and will never leave me alone.

And how can I forget, on some winter nights, a time when most of the birds have ceased their singing, and the coyotes have ceased their howling in the woods, all is quiet. A quiet little voice creeps in and tries to tell me I am alone, but then when I peek through the window and gaze up at the sky and see the many stars dancing, bobbing, and weaving from above, again I am reminded I am not alone.

And most of all, during the spring and summer nights, I hear my favorite birds, the whip-poor-wills, singing into the night, in their own language with a voice that penetrates the air from far and near, telling me that God loves me, with unfailing love, and He is always near and will never leave me alone. (*now leaning back in his favorite porch chair with a sense of calmness and peace on his face as he whispered with a soft voice that had a fading audibility*):

No, I am never alone.

No, I am never alone.

DAVID: (*after hearing Mr. Bill cite his many testimonial reasons why he never feels alone, he was so convinced that he too should never feel alone*) How can I ever thank you for your powerful and touching testimony of why you never feel like you are alone? Surely it is a reminder that I should never feel alone.

Suddenly David saw Priscilla, his wife, Jonathan, his son, and Ashley, Jonathan's fiancée, coming back from the town of Butler.

Mr. Bill, now after having developed a strong trust in David, anxiously waited to invite David's family back to his house. This time with a more relaxed accommodation.

Mr. Bill: I am looking forward to seeing them again.

A moment of special bonding between David's family and Mr. Bill

David: As soon as his family car arrived back at Mr. Bill's house, David met them at the car with Mr. Bill following closely behind. He quickly reminded them he was so glad to see them. After this, he reintroduced Priscilla, his wife, Jonathan, his son, and Ashley, his future daughter-in-law, to Mr. Bill.

Mr. Bill: (*seizing the moment*) Welcome back to my house. I look forward to getting to know you all better. Oh, by the way, David and I had a wonderful dialogue and observation session about the whip-poor-will birds and many other things. We both have grown in knowledge of the whip-poor-will by sharing our varied experiences with each other. And I know he can't wait to share it with you.

Priscilla: (*hearing the word* whip-poor-will *mentioned, with much excitement in her voice*) While we were visiting with our family in Butler, one of them shared some interesting information about the whip-poor-will.

David: (*quickly interjecting*) What did she say about the whip-poor-will?

Priscilla: Your cousin Isabelle told me she got a rare chance to see a whip-poor-will just a few nights before we arrived. It occurred as she was driving down a country road near her house, just as it was getting dark. Late that evening, her car lights reflected into the eyes of a bird that had ruby-red shining eyes as it looked into the car's headlights. As she drew closer to it, she recognized that it was a whip-poor-will bird searching for insects to eat.

MR. BILL: (*with a satisfying smile on his face*) I thank you for that wonderful information. For it confirms what I have been told by several other bird-watchers over the years that the chuck-will's-widow's eyes have a ruby-red glow when a car or flashlight shines on them. By the way, you perhaps recall I and other bird-watchers in this neck of the woods say the chuck-will's-widow is a first cousin of the eastern whip-poor-will?

DAVID: Thanks, Priscilla, for sharing this information with us the fact you indicated that Cousin Isabelle also confirmed that she was able to see that it was a whip-poor-will gives us additional information for better identifying a whip-poor-will.

MR. BILL: (*suddenly realizing it was getting late in the evening and anxious to bring David's son, Jonathan, into the conversation before ending their time together*) Jonathan, I am happy to hear that you have accompanied your father and mother on many occasions to Alabama.

JONATHAN: Yes, that is true, and I have always looked forward to traveling with my father and mother on our Alabama vacations. Over the years, it has helped me to appreciate my family background. Both my father and mother have always encouraged me to always connect to our family, including our extended family. And the importance of knowing that family is the essence of our identity. And of course, by now, after meeting with my father, I am sure you have discovered that he loves the outdoors, and one of his *pet projects* is finding out more about animals, and birds in general, and one of his main interests is learning more about the whip-poor-will.

MR. BILL: Jonathan, I am glad to hear that you enjoy coming to Alabama with your father and mother. By the way, I know this might sound a little selfish, but I must say that this trip I hope is as special to you as it is to me. For it has been a rewarding experience to dialogue with your father as we shared our individual experiences about outdoor life, and the whip-poor-will in particular. It has been a rewarding experience to share my practical knowledge with his book-learning knowledge. Because of this, we have grown in knowledge together. And Jonathan, I am confident that he will share this accumulated knowledge with you, and that you will be able to use it as you allow God to use you in continuing the *journey of searching for the whip-poor-will love song.*

JONATHAN: Thanks for that encouragement. Indeed, I, too, have come to have a hunger to learn more about the whip-poor-will and pass my information on to the next generation.

MR. BILL: Jonathan, I was happy to hear from your father that he and your mother were planning on retiring in the near future and coming back to Alabama to live. I was also happy to hear that you will be graduating from college next year. What are you studying in college? And what are your plans for the near future?

JONATHAN: Well, first of all, allow me to formally introduce you to my fiancée, Ashley, who will also be graduating from college next year. Ashley, meet Mr. Bill, one whom my grandfather, and now my father, have had occasion to dialogue with at great length.

ASHLEY: Mr. Bill, it is a pleasure meeting you, and we hope this will not be the last time.

MR. BILL: Ashley, it is a pleasure to meet you, and remember, you all are welcome to come and visit me again. (*he turned his attention back to Jonathan*) Now tell me about what you are studying in college.

JONATHAN: I am pleased to do so. I plan to receive a degree in business administration, with a minor in marketing. And now, I will ask Ashley to tell you what she is studying in college.

ASHLEY: Yes, I will be pleased to do so. I plan to receive a degree in English education, with a minor in music and theater production.

MR. BILL: My, my! It sounds like the type of technical and educational training that you and Jonathan are getting will be an ideal mix with the information that has been compiled by Jonathan's family to continue to seek and search for the whip-poor-will love song and what it is really singing.

When David heard Mr. Bill insert the whip-poor-will and its love song into the conversation, he now knew, without a doubt, that God had brought his family together with Mr. Bill.

DAVID: (*with a smile of satisfaction on his face*) Mr. Bill, how can I ever thank you enough for allowing me to interview you today and record it also? Also, I want to thank you for meeting and dialoguing with my wife Anne, my son Jonathan, and his fiancée, Ashley. And lest I forget, I am confident that together we, as a team, will be successful as we continue our journey: *in search of the whip-poor-will love song.*

MR. BILL: David, how can I ever forget to remind you that this has been one of the best days of my life? I will always treasure the time I spent with you and your family. I feel like God has brought us together for a special purpose. So remember, you and your family are always welcome to come and visit me again.

DAVID: Likewise, this too has been one of the most rewarding days in my life. And my family and I hope to see you again in the very near future.

Now David and family, each individually gave Mr. Bill a warm hug and gathered into their car and waved goodbye to him.

As Mr. Bill watched their car leave his yard, he waved at them with tears in his eyes. Deep down inside he knew that he, David, and his family had become a team *in search of the whip-poor-will love song.*

CHAPTER 9

In Search of the Whip-poor-will Love Song within the Framework of the Millenium Generation (1980–1995)

Like preceding generations, millennials also carry over some of the value systems from past generations, while at the same time being influenced by value systems introduced in their current generation. However, like other generations, millennials display unique traits that make them different from their predecessors.

What are some unique traits that make millennials different from their predecessors?

Most social scientists agree that there are six characteristics of millennials that make them different from their predecessors:

- **They are more technologically savvy.** They are exposed to new technology that has grown exponentially in the last twenty years, such as the Internet, cell phones, iPhones, and social network media. They not only depend on technology; the technology even becomes part of their life. And based on the new technologies, millennials more readily communicate with others and obtain information quickly.
- **They have a greater cultural acceptance.** Millennials are more apt to accept different things. They are able to work

with other people easily and accept diverse cultures. The millennial generation is more tolerant of different races and religions.

— **Aided by technology, they have greater flexibility and are generally more able to multitask.** Although they do not expect to change, they are more readily able to accommodate new things and people.

— **They tend to be more independent.** The millennial generation is more likely to do things according to their own approach, but this does not mean that this generation prefers to work alone. However, they want to be able to propose their ideas and thoughts about the assigned task. Millennials consider themselves as being confident in dealing with tasks because of the availability of technology resources. In essence, technology is the reason they are independent.

— **They value teamwork.** Although millennials tend to show independence, however, they also readily participate in teamwork where they work together in a group to implement certain tasks. The millennials value the importance of teamwork because it allows each other to obtain more opinions from discussion or brainstorming. In other words, the millennial generation tends to prefer collaborating and working as a group to working alone.

— **Millennials are considered the entitlement generation.** Entitlement refers to this generation having a sense of hope in climbing the career ladder at a rate that would seem unreasonable to their colleagues of prior generations. As a consequence, when their expectations are not attained, the millennial generation will search for new opportunities. In essence, they want to move quickly up the ladder. One reason for this type of behavior is because increasingly we are taught in Western culture to have a sense of "me, myself, and I" attitude, one that is called individualism. Another reason for this type of behavior stems from the fact that workers have more latitude in selecting a job and its location than ever before.

Although one could give much credence to these six observations as to what makes the millennials different from other prior generations, the changes in Christian values or the lack thereof cannot be overlooked when comparing the millennials' values with those of prior generations. Case in point, according to Pew Research polls and other surveys, in the United States, Christian affiliation continues to decline at a rapid rate, and the increase of "nonreligious affiliation" is rising. It is indicated that adults under the age of 30 (25 percent) are unaffiliated, describing their religion as "atheist," "agnostic," or "nothing in particular." Only 18 percent of millennials currently report they attend religious services weekly or nearly weekly.

Of course, we must understand there are several key reasons causing this increasing trend of Christianity or other religions' nonreligious affiliation to take place:

1. the removal of prayer and Bible teaching from our schools and other public sectors;
2. the number of young people attending Sunday school or youth Bible studies in our churches are steadily declining;
3. In place of the Creation theory, the evolutionary theory is being taught in our schools. As a result, the majority of our youth are becoming, at an increasing rate, more biblically illiterate. With this in mind, one can easily understand why our youth, on an increasing basis, are hindered from readily learning how to have a personal relationship with God and being able to use the Bible as their arbiter in every aspect of life.

This is the environment that has influenced Jonathan's life values. However, Jonathan was fortunate in that he grew up in a religious family, one that has always exposed him to Christian values and how to love God and one another. Notwithstanding, he has also been exposed to non-Christian values that millennials have generally adopted, yet because of his close relationship with his grandparents, he has held on to many of his Christian values that will influence him throughout his life. Having said this, Jonathan is well prepared to take up the banner and take the lead in continuing the *search for the whip-poor-will love song.*

David is now ready to set the stage for passing on the banner to Jonathan to take the lead in searching for the whip-poor-will love song

David and Priscilla were now preparing to retire from their jobs and subsequently move to Alabama to live. At this juncture in life, David was pleased in knowing that over the last thirty years, he had focused on learning and compiling information about the whip-poor-will and its behavior in nearly every conceivable related area. Thanks to his father and mother who passed on to him the catalog of information they had compiled during their lifetime and thanks to them for encouraging and giving him the charge to continue the search for more information about the whip-poor-will and its love song. And thanks to his teachers, friends, his students, and all who shared with him what they knew about the whip-poor-will. Now it was time for him to pass the banner of continuing the search for the whip-poor-will love song to his son, Jonathan.

Charging and encouraging Jonathan and Ashley to continue the search for the whip-poor-will love song

David and Priscilla were pleased to know that Jonathan and his fiancée, Ashley, would be graduating from college in a few months. They were also pleased to learn that the couple planned on getting married shortly after graduation. Along with this, David and Priscilla were very much aware that Jonathan and Ashley would make an ideal team in continuing the search for the whip-poor-will love song. They were confident that their fields of study and the subsequent degrees each would receive would complement each other as a team in the endeavor to learn more about the whip-poor-will and its love song.

After returning to Long Island, New York, David sensed it was now time to sit down with Jonathan and encourage him to take the lead in continuing the search for the whip-poor-will love song. As David and Priscilla gathered together on this special day to meet with Jonathan and his fiancée, Ashley, they knew it was very important to give Jonathan a final review of the information they had compiled over many years as a result of searching for information about the whip-poor-will and its love song.

**Preparing Jonathan to take the lead in continuing
the search for the whip-poor-will love song**

DAVID: You and I have had many discussions about the whip-poor-will. And certainly, you have observed me over the past twenty-two years obtaining as much information as I could about the whip-poor-will through interviewing and dialoguing with others who had gained special interest in the whip-poor-will.

JONATHAN: Daddy, how can I forget the many conversations you and I had over the years about the whip-poor-will and the many times you reminded me how your father and mother passed on the banner to you to continue searching for the whip-poor-will and its love song? It is clear that you have, over the years, noticed that I, too, have a special interest in birds, especially the whip-poor-will.

DAVID: Yes, it is true, Jonathan, that over the years you have shown me that you have developed a special interest in birds.

JONATHAN: Much of this must be credited to you. As you know, Dad, over the years, even here on Long Island where we live, I recall at an early age that I was allowed to keep birds in our special bird cages in our den area.

DAVID: Yes, I remember how you kept several pet birds in our den. Of course, your favorite one was the parrot. And even today, you have one in our house here on Long Island.

JONATHAN: True. In fact, from childhood, and even now, we have always had a parrot in our house. Clearly, the Amazon parrot is one of our favorite pet birds. They are good company due to their playful and outgoing nature. They enjoy being the center of attention and are known for their singing and talking. The parrot is a keen observer and likes to imitate one's vocal sound and one's movements as well. In fact, we must confess we had to learn not to use swear words around our parrot because it would conveniently repeat words you say, and sometimes inconveniently when we have company.

DAVID: (*with a chuckle and smile on his face*) It trained us well. For it taught us to be careful what we say around the parrot, and as a carryover, it taught us to be careful what we say around other people.

JONATHAN: Come to think of it, it was like having a mysterious person in our house. While we're on the subject of birds, I would be remiss if I did not mention the many times you took us to the numerous bird sanctuaries on the eastern part of Long Island to observe the many types of birds, as well as name as many as we could. (*as an afterthought*) By the way, I can never recall seeing or hearing a whip-poor-will on Long Island.

DAVID: One reason for this is because Long Island is increasingly becoming more densely populated by reason of the influx of many people who formerly lived in New York City, opting to move to Long Island because of its suburban settings which has the Long Island Sound on its north shore and the Atlantic Ocean on its south shore. The great influx of people has created an increasing demand for more housing, offices, businesses, and other needs that require additional space. As a result, Long Island's farmland and forest land are rapidly disappearing, meaning that the bird habitation areas are disappearing.

JONATHAN: Daddy, one thing for sure, this did not stop you from going where the birds are plentiful. I cannot count the many times you took us on excursions to the Upstate New York areas such as the Catskills and Poconos which have plenty of forest land. As I look back on my youth days, I now, more and more, appreciate the vast amount of knowledge and information we all gained in the process of being exposed to outdoor life that included fishing, hiking, and visiting many wildlife habitats, to name a few. And most of all, how can I forget, during the spring breaks from school, and during the summer, when school was out, the many trips we made to Alabama to visit family, cousins, and others in your hometown area? This was a time you also made sure our family used these visits to enjoy the outdoor life, fishing, swimming, and most of all listening to the whip-poor-will sing its love song at night.

DAVID: That's true, Jonathan. I must confess, although we have lived a good life on Long Island, with its beautiful beaches on the south shoreside, next to the Atlantic Ocean, as well as on the North shoreside, next to the Long Island Sound, I have always had a longing to go back to Alabama and live. (*with a smile on his face, saying in a hintingly way*) You can take a boy out of the country, but you can't take the country out of the boy.

PRISCILLA: (*in a way of* piggybacking *on what David said, with an affirming smile on her face*) I too have always enjoyed the many wonderful trips we made to Alabama.

ASHLEY, JONATHAN'S FIANCÉE: (*sensing this was a good time for her to interject also, with an accommodating smile on her face*) Although this was my first time traveling to Alabama, I have enjoyed my time there as we visited with your friendly family members and friends and observed the peaceful surroundings. It somewhat reminds me of the rural town where I grew up, Upstate New York. And of course, I must not forget the hospitality that Mr. Bill showed us. It was clear he was so pleased to have the honor of sharing with Mr. David his experience during their long discussion about the whip-poor-will and related information.

DAVID: (*with an even more satisfying smile on his face*) I am happy to hear that you enjoyed your trip to Alabama with us.

ASHLEY: (*nodding with an assuring smile on her face*) Thank you.

DAVID: (*sensing that it was time to reinforce that he and Priscilla have agreed they would be moving to Alabama after they both retire from their current jobs, as he said with a solemn tone while looking into Jonathan's eyes*) Jonathan, we have observed over the years that you have always had a special interest in birds and animals in general. Moreover, the fields of study you and Ashley have undertaken, in our opinion, will complement each other as a team in the final stages of searching for the whip-poor-will love song.

JONATHAN AND ASHLEY: (*as Jonathan and Ashley held hands, they both looked in the direction of David and Priscilla and nodded in agreement* as they said) We will do our very best in completing the final stages of searching for the whip-poor-will love song.

DAVID: (*with a smile of satisfaction on his face*) We are confident that the two of you will do a great job, especially knowing that as a result of your field of studies in college, and in the process of which you have also learned how to use the new technological tools that are at your disposal. Additionally, you will be able to use all the information that your grandparents, as well as all the information Priscilla and I have cataloged and compiled over many years, which we are confident will give you much background information about the whip-poor-will, its special attributes, its behavioral patterns, and the mystery of its song.

JONATHAN: Daddy, over the years I have been privileged to have many discussions with you about practically every aspect of the whip-poor-will and your search for the meaning of the whip-poor-will love song. I stand ready to continue the search that you and your grandparents began many years ago.

DAVID: I am confident that you and Ashley will meet with success in this endeavor. Priscilla and I want you to know that we are retiring from our jobs soon, and afterward, we plan on moving to Alabama to live in our retirement. However, please remember we will always be available to assist you all in any way. Remember: the bird is in your hand.

JONATHAN: Thanks, Dad, for the encouragement in knowing that you all will be there to support us. And, yes, I read you: the bird is in my hand.

CHAPTER 10

JONATHAN FOCUSES ON HIS INITIAL CHALLENGES IN CONTINUING THE SEARCH FOR THE WHIP-POOR-WILL LOVE SONG

Jonathan, after hearing that his parents were planning on retiring and moving to Alabama to live soon, realized that his and Ashley's immediate days ahead would be filled with demanding transitions. In addition, he also knew that he and Ashley planned to marry soon after they graduated from college in a few months. Meanwhile, for the time being, he knew that it was critically important for him to take inventory of what he needed to do in his quest to continue the search for the whip-poor-will love song before traveling to Alabama with his parents for the upcoming spring break from school.

Knowing that early spring in Alabama was an ideal time to hear the whip-poor-wills sing during the night, he also knew that this was an ideal time for the whip-poor-wills to be in their nesting stage. So he quickly ran through his mind the main achievements he intended to accomplish while in Alabama:

1. Obtain a close-up recording of the whip-poor-will love song.
2. Obtain close-up pictures of the whip-poor-will during the day when it is mainly sleeping, or at night when they become active.

3. Make an in-wood search for one of their nests and hopefully find one of the adults sitting on eggs in it, or better yet, find a nest with little hatchlings in it.

With this in mind, he knew that at minimum he needed to purchase some special equipment:

1. a high-quality digital recorder that could record the whip-poor-wills singing;
2. a high-quality digital camera for capturing pictures of birds and other wild animals;
3. digital binoculars with night vision capability;
4. two pairs of snake boots; and
5. a special snake gun, to be used in case there is an encounter with a dangerous snake.

Jonathan reflects on all the things his father has taught him about outdoor activities

As Jonathan reflected on all the things his father had taught him about outdoor activities, he now realized that he was being prepared for such a time as this. He would be forever grateful for all the things his father had taught him about outdoor activities such as wild game hunting and how to cast a reel and rod on their many fishing trips.

In addition, his father, who was a Korean War veteran, reminded him that during military service, he was taught how to shoot weapons from different shooting positions, for example, shooting from a standing position, shooting from a kneeling position, and shooting from a prone position. His father also reminded him he learned many of these shooting techniques from reading Western comic books and watching cowboy movies, one of his favorite pastimes, during his youth days.

As he reflected on how his father had passed on these skills to him, he knew that his father had taught him well in gaining real-life experiences. And now he realized he would be taking the lead role in searching for the whip-poor-will and its love song. He was fully aware it would require him to spend many precious hours in the woods of Alabama. And as a result, he might be called upon to use a gun to defend himself.

Jonathan now takes the lead in searching for the whip-poor-will love song in Alabama

Loaded with the necessary equipment he had earlier decided to use in his search for the whip-poor-will love song, Jonathan and Ashley, along with his parents, were now back in Alabama during their spring school break. It was now mid-April, a time when the whip-poor-wills are singing in great numbers. Not only this, Jonathan had learned that the whip-poor-wills were now actively in their nesting season, a time when they are nesting on their eggs.

During the day, they cannot be heard or seen out in the open. Knowing that whip-poor-wills are nocturnal birds. Jonathan fully understood that they rest on the ground or horizontally on a low tree branch, sleeping most of the daylight hours. However, he knew that beginning in early spring and throughout most of the summer months, their singing can be heard from miles around, beginning late evening when the evening shadows begin to give way to darkness.

Now Jonathan and Ashley, along with their parents, were sitting in chairs on the wraparound porch of their family home in Alabama. They could smell the sweet fragrance of early spring flowers and other assorted plants and trees during their early sprouting time. As the sweet southern breeze caressed their faces, darkness was beginning to creep in. Suddenly, they began hearing whip-poor-wills singing in the distance. Their singing became louder as they came nearer to where they were sitting. However, it was now too dark for them to be seen. Nevertheless, Jonathan had been taught to notice how the whip-poor-will nearby began singing at one location for a while and then incessantly moved to another location and sing.

As his father had taught him: if their locations are noticed carefully as they move from station to station, you can establish the pattern of their circuit and thereby get a good idea of the approximate location of their nesting area. For Jonathan, this bit of information was important to know if he was to find a good location to get a close-up recording of a whip-poor-will singing. This was key to Jonathan because getting a close-up and quality recording of their singing was his number one priority on his list if he was to analyze what they were singing.

He and his family continued to listen to the whip-poor-wills sing from 8:00 p.m. to about 10:00 p.m. Now he was confident he had a good idea of where to station his recorder to get a close-up recording of a whip-poor-will singing the next day. As he pondered this with anticipation throughout the night, needless to say, he did not sleep much that night.

Jonathan and Ashley successfully obtained a recording of whip-poor-wills singing

After eating breakfast with his family, Jonathan reminded his father and mother that he and Ashley planned to locate a tape recorder in one of the low-branch trees near where he had heard a whip-poor-will singing the night before. His parents nodded in agreement that it would be a great idea. After that, his parents reminded him they would be visiting other family members in town for most of the day.

DAVID: (*with a smile on his face*) I am confident that you will be successful in your endeavor. Remember, the bird is in your hand.
JONATHAN: (*smiled in affirmation*) Yes, the bird is in my hand.

Throughout the day, Jonathan and Ashley preplanned how they would prepare for their all-important recording excursion. They decided it was important to take with them, first and foremost, the special tape recorder, and of course, a snake pistol for defense against a possible snake encounter, and a pair of snake-proof boots for each one to wear.

It was now approximately 7:00 p.m., Jonathan and Ashley traveled to the area where they had heard a whip-poor-will singing the night before. After arriving at the general area where they decided would be the best spot to stake out their tape recorder, they readied for the next step. Jonathan took the lead along the way with Ashley carefully following; soon, they were able to locate what they thought would be an ideal location. It was near an open area next to several low-branch trees. After deciding on the tree they would use, Jonathan opened the strap on the camera and wrapped it around the selected tree, approximately five feet above ground level. Making sure his recorder was turned on with the proper adjustment, he quietly whispered to Ashley.

JONATHAN: This is our big moment.
ASHLEY: Yes, indeed, this surely will be one of the highlights in searching for the whip-poor-will love song.

Jonathan and Ashley carefully left the area traveled back to the family home and quietly sat on the front porch to wait for the precious moment for a whip-poor-will to start singing. The evening shadows were beginning to give way to darkness.

While sitting there, it was amazing how many other sounds they were able to decipher while they waited. They could hear a mourning dove in the distance; they were able to hear many other birds singing or tweeting their usual songs as each of them traveled to their roosting places before dark. Jonathan had been taught by his father to identify some birds by the sounds or songs they make. For example, he was quite sure that the thrasher, the mockingbird, the warbler, the red cardinal bird, the house wren, and even the blue jay bird were among them. And Ashley, having grown up in a rural area in Upstate New York, was able to identify many of these also.

During their time sitting there, it was amazing how many other sounds they could hear. For instance, they could hear a dog barking from almost a mile away. In addition, they were able to hear an airplane flying overhead and cars and trucks making their usual sounds as they traveled to and from their destinations. With this in mind, they nodded at each other.

JONATHAN: It looks like we might be able not only to be able to record whip-poor-wills singing but also, his surrounding company of *friends* in concert with him.
ASHLEY: This is exciting in and of itself.

Now it was approximately 7:45 p.m. By now the shadows had given way to darkness. Suddenly, they heard the sound of whip-poor-wills singing in the distance. Eventually, they were able to hear one singing louder and louder as it was alternately singing incessantly as it moved to another location.

Finally, the singing got louder as it moved closer to where the tape recorder was located. As a result, both of their hearts began beating faster as they anticipated it moving closer and closer to the tape recorder. The whip-poor-will singing became louder and louder as it appeared to stop at a location near the tape recorder. As they gazed at their watches, to time the length of its singing, they discovered the whip-poor-will sang for about ten minutes before moving to a new location. They both looked at each other.

ASHLEY: I, myself, have never been this close to a whip-poor-will singing.
JONATHAN: (nodding in agreement) Neither have I.

They happily smiled at each other as they agreed. Surely the whip-poor-will was singing about something other than its name.

After waiting for another fifteen minutes or so, the sound of the whip-poor-will began fading away. At this point, Jonathan, with a flashlight in hand, accompanied by Ashley, had now decided to go into the wooded area and retrieve the tape recorder from the tree it was attached to. As they headed back to the family home with the tape recorder in hand, Jonathan, with a confident smile on his face, looked at Ashley as he said it had been a good day, to which Ashley agreed.

Jonathan now took the tape recorder and carefully pressed the rewind button to rewind it back to the beginning of the tape. After which, he carefully pressed the play button. Right away he knew the recording was successful, just by listening to the beginning of it he recorded all the sounds of other birds singing and other *accompanying friends*, prior to the main attraction, the whip-poor-wills in concert.

As they sat there and listened until the tape recording reached the area that began recording the whip-poor-will singing, they were even more convinced than ever before that the whip-poor-will was singing something other than its name. Jonathan, now after carefully making sure he was touching the right button, pushed the power-off button and carefully placed the tape recorder in a bag. With the bag secured on his shoulder, he and Ashley headed back to the family home; they could hardly wait to share the recording with his parents.

While sitting on the front porch of the family home, they soon heard a car coming in the distance. As it got closer, Jonathan could see the silhouette of its shape; it appeared to be his parents returning to the family home. Upon arriving near the porch of the family home and parking their car, David and Priscilla hurriedly came to the porch where Jonathan and Ashley were sitting in the porch swing as they swayed back and forth.

David immediately could tell by the satisfying look on their faces that they were anxious to share the good news.

DAVID: (*with a curious smile on his face*) Was your recording excursion successful?

JONATHAN: Yes, beyond and above what we had expected.

PRISCILLA: How so?

JONATHAN: Mother, the good news is that our tape recorder was not only able to record a whip-poor-will singing close up but in addition, prior to the whip-poor-will's singing, it was able to record songs of other birds as well as other surprising sounds. It was like listening to the whip-poor-will in concert with his *accompanying friends.*

PRISCILLA: (*with excitement in her voice*) I cannot wait to hear it. However, I suggest we eat supper first, and afterward, we can listen to the recording.

JONATHAN: Sounds okay to me, and I am sure Ashley likewise will agree.

Ashley, with an accommodating smile on her face, nodded in agreement. Jonathan's mother indicated they had brought more than enough food from their cousin's house, who insisted that they take enough food for all of us and more. David, upon hearing Priscilla mentioning food, beckoned Jonathan to assist him in bringing the food from the car into the family house dining room.

As they feasted on the food, David reminded Jonathan and Ashley they had a wonderful time visiting their cousins and others in the community.

DAVID: By the way, they reminded us they are looking forward to seeing you and Ashley while we are in town.

JONATHAN: (*with an assuring smile on his face*) Indeed, my trip to Alabama would not be complete unless I visit with my cousins and others in the community. It will be an honor to introduce Ashley to them.

After they finished supper, they agreed it was a good time to go into the family den area and prepare to listen to the recording that Jonathan had successfully made during their excursion in searching for the whip-poor-will song. After each one found a comfortable seating place, Jonathan placed the recorder on a table nearby; and after making sure the tape had rewound to its starting position, he turned it on.

Before pressing the play button, he made sure to remind his parents that the first part of the tape would play the recording of the other birds, and distant sounds prior to the whip-poor-will singing. His parents nodded, thanking David for giving them a preview of what was to occur.

Now for the special moment: he pressed the play button and returned to his seat nearby. After listening to the tape play the songs of other birds singing, in addition to other accompanying sounds for approximately thirty minutes, which was entertaining in and of itself, they could now hear the whip-poor-wills beginning to sing from a far distance from the tape recorder. Suddenly the sound of one whip-poor-will got louder and louder. They realized this was because it was getting closer to the tape recorder. Soon the sound had reached a loud and clear sound of the whip-poor-will singing.

As they sat on the edge of their seats, it had already become clear that the whip-poor-wills were singing something other than their name, whip-poor-will.

DAVID: (*with a sense of exuberance and in an excited voice*) This is a big deal, Jonathan. I want to give you and Ashley a big shout of congratulations. Your recording of the whip-poor-will song is surely one of the major milestones in our search for the whip-poor-will love song.

We all can speculate what it's saying. However, we know ultimately it will take someone who is able to amplify the tape's recording and afterward begin analyzing it with the proper tools and training.

PRISCILLA: (*with a big suggestive smile on her face as she looked at Jonathan and Ashley*) I am confident that the two of you, together with the training you have received in pursuing your degrees, are well capable of getting the job done.

Jonathan and Ashley looked at each other and then in David and Priscilla's direction as they promised they'd do their very best.

As an afterthought, Jonathan now realized that the recording he had made on his tape of the recording of the whip-poor-will love song was too precious to take a chance of losing it. With this in mind, he duplicated another copy of it on a separate recorder that he had the foresight to bring with him on their trip to Alabama. So he quickly reminded his parents that he was going to tape record a duplicate copy before going to bed.

Suddenly, the thought came to his mind that they had only a couple of days left on their spring break before traveling back to Long Island, New York.

JONATHAN: Ashley and I are planning on going back to the same general location where we made the successful recording earlier. We intend to do this tomorrow. This time, we plan to go during the daylight hours to search for a whip-poor-will nesting on its eggs. As you know, they sleep mostly during the daytime.

Therefore, we will be searching during the day in the hope of not only finding a whip-poor-will sitting on its nest during its nesting period but also taking pictures of the whip-poor-will. It is our plan to take pictures of the whip-poor-will, its eggs, or even the little hatchlings in the nest also.

After hearing Jonathan say this, David reminded Jonathan that he and Priscilla needed to go into town to take care of some business affairs tomorrow morning and that they hoped to return early afternoon.

DAVID: Meanwhile, we wish you much success in your search, but please be careful. (*with a concerned look on his face*) Just remember the things I taught you over the years about protecting yourself while hunting in the woods.

Jonathan looked at David and said with an appreciative gesture.

JONATHAN: I will, Dad. I will, Dad.
PRISCILLA: (*with a concerned smile on her face, looked at Jonathan and Ashley*) Please be careful!

Now it was time to say good night to each other before retiring to bed. Throughout the night, Jonathan did not get much sleep as a result of thinking about how he would approach his search for a whip-poor-will and its nest. He kept pondering the fact that he had already discovered it was possible that a nest could be found in the general area where he had recorded the whip-poor-will singing. With this in mind, he decided he would begin his search in this area.

Next, he thought about the equipment and special clothing he needed to wear. He also remembered what his father had told him: that some snakes also hunt birds, eggs, and even little chicks, etc., during the day. With this in mind, he knew he must take with him a snake gun that he and his father had packed for snake protection: a gun/pistol that fires.38 shot shells. He convinced himself that he would do a checklist of things he needed upon arising early in the morning. Having pondered over this, he was finally content that he was well prepared, preplanning, equipment-wise, and with loads of confidence.

Upon awakening the next morning, he and his father sat on the front porch sipping morning coffee, while his mother and Ashley prepared breakfast. Soon breakfast was ready and all gathered around the table in mutually arranged chairs. David blessed the food, after which each one filled their plate and began eating. As David looked at Jonathan, he recognized he had a faraway look on his face. Immediately, he recognized that look as one whose adrenaline was already on high alert. Knowing this, David and the others did not have much to say to each other, for they knew Jonathan was focused on the task ahead.

After rising from the breakfast table, David once again reminded Jonathan that he and his mother would be going into town shortly to take care of some family business. As he looked at Jonathan and then at Ashley, he encouraged and wished them a successful search that day. With a confident and determined countenance on his face, Jonathan said thanks for the encouragement.

Now it was approximately 9:00 a.m.; Jonathan and Ashley were sitting on the front porch finalizing a plan for the search. They agreed that he would begin his search, as a starting point, from the tree where he had located his recording of the whip-poor-will's singing the day before. Using this as a referencing point, he would use his GPS mapping equipment to plot grid lines that would encompass not more than a half-mile square area for his initial search. Next, they took inventory of equipment and gear needed for their search:

a. two pairs of snake boots;
b. a pair of binoculars;
c. a quality camera for taking pictures of birds; and
d. a gun/pistol that fires .38 shot shells.

Next, Jonathan and Ashley agreed that she would position herself near the starting point in an open space and wait there while he searched the general area plotted out by the GPS. They both agreed they each would have an iPhone with them to maintain contact with each other.

Convinced that they had covered all bases necessary for a safe and successful search, Jonathan and Ashley began walking to the location of their search, pleased that the day was sunny.

They noticed many beautiful wildflowers in full bloom as their sweet fragrance penetrated the soft southern breeze, which had a calming effect on them as they breathed in the sweet-smelling southern air. Jonathan and Ashley walked a short distance to the general location for the search. Ashley, as previously agreed, took her station in an open space near the tree where they had successfully recorded the whip-poor-will song the day before. They both had already agreed that she would remain there while Jonathan would venture into the wooded area to do the actual searching.

Jonathan and Ashley now compassionately looked at each other as they both embraced, followed by an affirming kiss. As he prepared to begin his search, Jonathan reminded Ashley that he would call her on the iPhone from time to time during his search. Ashley nodded with a somewhat anxious look on her face. As Jonathan began walking toward the wooded area, he turned and gave Ashley a thumbs-up sign. Ashley, with a somewhat concerned smile on her face, in return gave him a thumbs-up sign.

Now as Jonathan disappeared into the woods, he knew he was all alone, but not entirely alone, because he had faith that God was with him and would keep a *wall of protection around him.* He also knew there were many birds and animals in the woods. In fact, he had learned by studying birds and wild animals that they have a greater sense of smell, a greater sense of hearing, and a greater sense of seeing than human beings, which gives them the ability to see us before we see them.

Loaded down with equipment and necessary gear, he used a walking stick held in his hand to poke in the weeds and tall grass ahead of where he was walking. Knowing that whip-poor-wills mostly sleep on the ground or on a low tree limb during the day, he was very aware that with their camouflaging colors that gave them the ability to blend in with the leaves and grass, they were very difficult to locate. With this awareness, he was careful to use his binoculars to survey a circuit of the area around him as he slowly moved from one area to another.

Suddenly, he recalled what his father had told him about snakes hunting for bird eggs and even little baby chicks during the day. He also knew that he was near a bottom area with a creek nearby. For some reason, as he pondered this, he could not get this *snake thing* out of his mind. It was an eerie feeling.

Jonathan's encounter with a water moccasin/cottonmouth snake

As a result of this premonition, he checked his belt and holster and his snake pistol within, making sure the latch was loose so that he could quickly draw, as his father had taught him. Jonathan thought about what his father had told him about water moccasins. He indicated they are very territorial and can be very aggressive toward anyone or anything else infringing upon their territory. He also remembered that his father had told him that the water moccasin, the rattlesnake, among the list of other snakes, are poisonous and a bite from either one of them could be deadly if medical help cannot be gotten right away.

As he walked deeper into the woods, he noticed that birds and other animals upon seeing or hearing him would scamper away from him as they disappeared further into the woods. Suddenly, he heard a shuffling sound. It did not sound like a four-legged creature that made a skipping sound as it walked; neither did it sound like a rattlesnake, which often makes a rattling noise with its tail when feeling threatened. Rather, it was an incessant sound as if something was sliding through the leaves and grass. The sound got louder and louder.

As he turned around to look in the direction of the sound, he saw a water moccasin coming after him with its head raised off the ground, with its white cottonmouth wide open! As his father had taught him, he quickly drew the snake pistol from its holster, aimed directly at the target, and fired immediately, two rounds in succession. The snake instantly dropped its head, what was left of it, and fell to the ground and came to a standstill and appeared to be dead. He fired one more shot in the neck area. It has been said, "If you kill the head, the body will die." It was dead for sure.

Ashley, who was stationed a distance away in the opening, patiently waiting for Jonathan, heard the sound of shooting. She recognized it came from within the area where Jonathan was searching. Suddenly a feeling came upon her as she asked herself if he was alright. Immediately she picked up her iPhone and dialed Jonathan's number. Jonathan picked up his iPhone as it was ringing and said hello.

ASHLEY: Jonathan, Jonathan, are you alright?
JONATHAN: (*calmly answering*) Yes, Ashley, I am alright.
ASHLEY: I heard the shooting. What happened?
JONATHAN: I just shot and killed a water moccasin that tried to chase me, but don't worry, it will not chase anyone else because it is dead.
ASHLEY: (*with a sigh of relief*) Jonathan, are you okay?
JONATHAN: Yes, I am okay.
ASHLEY: Thank God you are okay, Jonathan. Please end your search!
JONATHAN: Yes, Ashley, I am ending my search. Just please stay where you are. I am coming out of the woods and heading your way.

As Jonathan came out from the wooded area, Ashley kept checking on him via her iPhone.

ASHLEY: Jonathan, where are you now?
JONATHAN: I am headed your way. Please relax. I am on my way.

Soon Ashley could hear shuffling in the woods as Jonathan was getting near where she was. Seconds later, she could see the silhouette of his body wearing the bright-orange hunting vest. As he was getting closer to her, she could see that he was walking with his usual strut, one of confidence. She was so happy and relieved to see him. So much so, she could not wait until he came to where she was waiting. Suddenly, with an overwhelming impulse, she ran to him and reached out with open arms thanking God he was okay. Jonathan, with a compassionate smile on his face, reached out to her with open arms. As they embraced, they both whispered to each other: "I love you."

ASHLEY: (*now with a confident smile on her face, looked at Jonathan*) You know what?
JONATHAN: What?
ASHLEY: (*looking at him with an encouraging smile*) Jonathan, you are a hero.
JONATHAN: It was because of God's grace, and what my father taught me, that I am safe and sound.

As they walked back to the family home, they both agreed that their searching expedition was successful by the mere fact that they were able to take the initiative to go out for the first time in search of a whip-poor-will and its nest. And in addition, they knew this would only be the beginning of their search for the whip-poor-will and its nest. Moreover, they both agreed that they had achieved their main goal the day before in which they were successful in obtaining a quality recording of the whip-poor-will love song.

Upon arriving back at the family house, they discovered that Jonathan's parents had already returned from their special trip to take care of needed business affairs. As Jonathan and Ashley approached the front porch where David's parents were sitting in their favorite country chairs enjoying the beautiful camellias, azaleas, wisteria, and other numerous wildflowers—and even some of which they could not name—each one giving off its unique fragrance that oozed through the soft southern breeze, the smell of which gave a combination of calmness, peace, and exhilaration, all in one.

Jonathan could not help noticing that David had a curious smile on his face, one that usually led to an all-important question.

DAVID: Were you successful in your search for a whip-poor-will and its nest?
JONATHAN: Yes and no.

DAVID: (*with an inquisitive look on his face*) What do you mean, yes or no?

JONATHAN: Well, let's put it this way. First of all, we were successful in the sense that we were able to make an initial search. However, our search was cut short by an unfriendly water moccasin.

DAVID: What happened?

JONATHAN: I had an encounter with a water moccasin that decided to chase after me. Thanks to you, Dad, for training me how to use a pistol. As I was walking in the woods searching for a whip-poor-will and its nest, a water moccasin chased after me. I quickly turned around and made a *quick draw* of the pistol from my holster, just like you taught me, and fired two shots aimed at the water moccasin's cotton mouth and killed it instantly.

PRISCILLA: (*overhearing the conversation*) I am happy that nothing happened to you. (*without hesitating, she made a motherly suggestion*) Jonathan, I suggest you end your search for now.

JONATHAN: (*looking at his mother and saying in an accommodating way*) Yes, Mom, I will. I will. (*with a special smile on his face, he looked at Ashley*) Ashley has made the same suggestion. And we mutually agreed that this would be the end of our search for now. And by the way, we both agreed that the successful recording of the whip-poor-will love song yesterday was our primary goal and that the recording is the major source that will provide us with the most critical information for determining the message and wording of the whip-poor-will love song.

David reminded everyone that they had only two days left on their spring vacation. Jonathan replied that he was aware of this. He reminded them that he and Ashley had one more important trip to make before heading back to New York. Suddenly, David remembered the promise they had made to Mr. Bill (the wise old man) during their trip to Alabama last year.

JONATHAN: Daddy, you must be reading my mind about the promise made to Mr. Bill to visit him upon returning to Alabama. That's exactly what I had in mind.

David and his family have now arrived back in New York

Now that David and his family had arrived back in New York, it was time to begin taking inventory of all the major activities within the next several months that lay ahead for his family:

1. David and Anne's retirement;
2. Jonathan and Ashley's graduation from college;
3. Jonathan and Ashley's wedding date; and
4. in the interim, the analysis and interpretation of the whip-poor-will love song.

It was an exciting time in each of their lives. And of course, within these major activities, Jonathan and Ashley knew they must take the initiative in continuing to set the stage for analyzing and interpreting the recording that he and Ashley had successfully made of the whip-poor-will love song.

With this in mind, Jonathan and Ashley agreed that they must choose a recording studio to make an amplified version of the recording they had successfully made. They immediately began searching for different recording agencies in the Long Island area, as well as in the New York City area. They were successful in locating a company on Long Island that could tape an amplified version of their recording and also produce a sound wavelength of it. The recording studio promised to finish two amplified copies and several copies of the sound wavelength in approximately two weeks.

Ashley pondered what she needed to do in getting ready for graduation in a few months, and afterward plan for a wedding, yet the whip-poor-will song dominated her pondering the most.

Ashley ponders on how her majoring in English education could be used to help analyze and interpret the whip-poor-will love song

As she thought about her studying in preparation for a degree in English education, she recalled having learned about linguistics, the study of the nature and structure of human speech, and that it not only considers its structure, but also its grammar, syntax, and phonetics.

In particular, she knew that phonetics, which is the study of the sounds of speech, would play a critical part in determining, that is interpreting the words the whip-poor-will is using in its song.

Finally, she knew that she had to write this information down and mentally be prepared to use it when the amplified version of the recording was ready to use. She quietly said to herself that this was what she would share with Jonathan's family when they would sit down together in a joint session and began analyzing the whip-poor-will song recording.

Jonathan pondered on how he would connect what he hears on the whip-poor-will song recording to love

While waiting on the tape-recording agency to complete the copying of an amplified version of their recorded version of the whip-poor-will song, Jonathan began pondering what he had read in his grandfather's journal that had been passed on to David and afterward had been passed on to him. And he also knew he had other information his father had passed on to him, especially the recorded version of the interview his father had with Mr. Bill (the wise old man).

In a cursory reading/scanning through all the information on hand, he discovered a common theme that both his grandfather and Mr. Bill adhered to: each one emphasized that the whip-poor-will is singing something about love, and it also shows us that love is what love does.

With this bit of key information, he was confident that whatever the wording of the whip-poor-will recording is discovered, it invariably is connected to love.

CHAPTER 11

DAVID'S FAMILY JOINS IN A JOINT DIALOGUING SESSION TO BEGIN LISTENING TO THE AMPLIFIED VERSION OF THE WHIP-POOR-WILL SONG RECORDING

Having listened to the original version of the whip-poor-will song recording, each member of the family noted the total recording time of it. In addition, they knew the following:

1. The recording took place in late April, beginning about 7:20 p.m., during the evening time as daylight was beginning to give way to night, somewhere in Choctaw County, Alabama.
2. Jonathan and his family were aware that the first forty minutes or so consisted of recording other sounds that included the following: unnamed birds, the mourning dove, the sound of the wind, the sound of airplanes flying above, the sounds of cars and other vehicles passing by on a county road nearby, the sound of barking dogs, etc., and they were aware this, by and large, occurred prior to the singing of the whip-poor-wills, the main attraction, at about the forty-minute mark.

Analyzing the main attraction, the whip-poor-wills' singing

At first, the singing of the whip-poor-wills began at a distance from the recording station; their singing was very faint. This meant one could not hear the words of the song; and therefore, could not determine the syllables thereof. Think about it, this, in and of itself, helps to explain that many who hear the whip-poor-will sing do so from a distance too far off to accurately decipher what it is singing. As a result, this helps us to explain why some simply think it is singing its name, whip-poor-will, or singing some other phrase such as "Chip fell out the oak tree" or as some, suggesting in a funny way, say it is singing, "Whip her or I will."

As Jonathan and his family kept listening to the whip-poor-wills sing, it became clear that the closer it came to the recording station the clearer the wording of its singing became. Suddenly, one of the whip-poor-wills came very close to the tape recorder, which was attached to a tree (the recording station). After singing for a few minutes at this location, the whip-poor-will began moving away from the tape recorder; the further it moved from the tape recorder, the less distinguishable its song became. Also, Jonathan and his family noticed that there was more than one whip-poor-will singing within its designated circuit. The whip-poor-will's singing, as the tape recorder indicated, lasted about twenty minutes. Each one: David, Priscilla, Jonathan, and Ashley took notes as they were listening. After listening to the recording together, they agreed that each one would listen to it again.

Only this time, each one would have the opportunity to listen to the recording separately in order to give each one the option to independently press the pause and play button as necessary. Of course, this would give each one the ability to take notes as necessary. They agreed to meet again in two days and join together in a brainstorming session.

The brainstorming session

Two days have now passed. Each of the family members had been given an opportunity to listen to the recording of the whip-poor-will song alone and take necessary mental notes, as well as written notes, to be used in the brainstorming session, and later in the dialoguing and observation session. At the opening session of the brainstorming session, the family voted unanimously for David to serve as the facilitator. He accepted. However, from the outset, he reminded them that he would only act as a facilitator in the sense of guiding and questioning the participants in the process of analyzing what the whip-poor-will is saying in its song. And within this process, he would be allowed to give his input. They all agreed that he would be allowed to give his input also. With the group's affirmation, David was now ready to set the guidelines for the brainstorming process.

DAVID: Remember, our primary goal is to determine what the whip-poor-will is singing. Please be reminded each one of us has listened to the recording several times as a group, and in addition, each one of us has listened to it several times alone. And in the process, each of us had the opportunity to take mental notes, as well as written notes.

However, in our brainstorming session today you will be required to write down in your notes the words you think the whip-poor-will is singing by listening to the recording for five minutes. And after which I will ask each one to call out the words they think the whip-poor-will is singing. I then will write them under each one's name on a screen projected on a lighted wall. Remember, the purpose of brainstorming is to give each one the opportunity to make their individual input freely, without the fear of rejection. So whatever words you think you hear, write it down, no matter how silly or funny it may sound to others. (*having an encouraging smile on his face*) Let the fun begin!

Again, David played the recording of the whip-poor-will song for another five minutes, and after pausing and giving each person time to finalize the list of their suggested wordings of the song, David began calling out each person's name, asking them to read out aloud their suggested wordings.

PRISCILLA: I heard three words: *hiss willy will.*
JONATHAN: (*yelling*) *Hiss really real.*
ASHLEY: (*yelling*) *It's really real.*

As each person yelled out the three suggested words they thought they heard, David wrote them down under each person's name and projected them on the screen. After which David thanked each one for his or her suggested list of words they think they hear in the song.

DAVID: Our next step is to sit and dialogue and observe with each other in a group discussion. (*initiating the dialoguing and obser-vation session*) We will begin with our first responder in list-ing her suggested three words of the whip-poor-will love song. Priscilla, why did you choose, the three words, *hiss willy will?*
PRISCILLA: Well, the first word (*hiss*), I chose simply sounded like something making a hissing sound. And the second and third words, *willy will,* I chose because they sounded like a person pronouncing words starting with the letter *r* sound as a *w* sound. With this in mind, one can see how *willy will* could be the same as *really real.* I am aware that there are some people who have difficulty pronouncing words starting with the letter *r.* (*Priscilla now looked in Ashley's direction*). Ashley, being that you are an English major in college, perhaps you can help me explain this to us in a more informed way.
ASHLEY: (*with an accommodating smile on her face*), Yes, one of my secondary areas of study in English was in the area of speech therapy. We call it *rhotacism.* Although the real cause of rho-tacism is unknown, it is believed to be linked to what we call tongue-tie. It is believed that tongue-tie may limit the range of tongue movements, which is critical for pronouncing the letter *r.*

PRISCILLA: Ashley, this reminds me of what one of my friends who took a vacation in Hawaii said. My friend told me, "While I was in Hawaii, I wanted to be sure I was pronouncing *Hawaii* right. So I asked another vacationer who was from Germany. I asked him, 'How do you pronounce Hawaii?' He replied by saying, '*Havaii.*' I responded by politely saying thank you. In kind, he responded by saying, 'You are *velcome.*'"

ASHLEY: (*Ashley, along with David and Jonathan, gave out a loud chuckle*) We all must remember people from different countries have what we call different accents. However, what we must remember is that people in some countries have unique nuances in their pronunciation. For example, some people from other countries pronounce the letter *i* with an *e* sound. However, Priscilla, we want you to know that what you think the whip-poor-will is saying in its song is to be commended, and in no way are we saying that you are making fun of the whip-poor-will.

PRISCILLA: Thank you, Ashley, for your encouragement. Indeed, I only suggested what my ears heard: *hiss willy will.*

DAVID: (*with an encouraging smile on his face*) Thank you, Priscilla and Ashley, for that wonderful input. It was both informational and funny. Next, we will hear from Jonathan. Jonathan, why did you choose "*hiss really real*"?

JONATHAN: (*with a smile that exuded confidence as he pondered his selection*), Well, I chose *hiss really real* because phonetically this is what my ears heard. I am not sure about the first word, *hiss.* However, we do know that birds and other animals often make a hissing sound.

DAVID: (*with an assuring smile*) Your selection, *hiss really real*, deserves consideration. I am sure your input will prove to be very valuable to our final analysis.

JONATHAN: (Thanks, Dad, for your encouragement.

DAVID: (*now looking toward Ashley*) Now we will hear from Ashley as she explains why she selected *It's really real.* And by the way, Ashley, please feel free to use your English background to help give us further understanding of the linguistic metrics such as phonetics, the syntax of sentence structures, and the impor-tance of breaking words into syllables, etc.

ASHLEY: (*with an accommodating smile on her face*) Mr. David, I thank you for giving me a list of key words we must under-stand when analyzing the sound of words. With this in mind, please be patient with me because explaining the meaning and usage of the list of key words you have listed will take careful examination.

PRISCILLA: (*with an affirming smile on her face*) Please take your time. We all understand that your input in this area is critical for us to better analyze the whip-poor-will love song.

ASHLEY: Thanks. Now let's look at some of the key words we need to focus on: linguistics, phonetics, syntax, and syllables of words. Here are their basic definitions:

- *Linguistics*—the study of the way in which language works and how it considers its structure, grammar, syntax, and phonetics.
- *Phonetics*—The study of speech sounds.
- *Syntax*—The order or arrangement of words and phrases to form a proper sentence.

Mr. David, you perhaps know that I had the privilege of reading the journal of information that you have collected and compiled concerning the whip-poor-will. And as a result, I took note of a particular statement you made.

Here is what you said about all of God's creation speak-ing to us in its own language: Although every aspect of God's creation speaks in its own language, whether it be in the form of praise, proclamation, moans, and groans, to man, these utterings are mostly unintelligible and therefore are not readily translated.

Certainly, we know the whip-poor-will is no exception. God is using it to speak to us in his own language. Of course, our task is to translate it into a language we can understand. And phonetically, I believe we can achieve this purpose by ana-lyzing its speech sounds. And by the way, Jonathan has made our job easier by being able to record a close-up recording of the whip-poor-will love song and subsequently obtaining an amplified version of the same. Thanks to Jonathan for a job well done.

Priscilla: (*now looking in Jonathan's direction*) You have made our job easier as we attempt to analyze what the whip-poor-will is singing to us.

Jonathan: (*with a smile of satisfaction on his face*) The marketing skills I acquired in college played a big role in my being able to successfully record the whip-poor-will love song. I couldn't have done it without the aid of Ashley. And let me add, I couldn't have done it without Dad and Mom exposing me to outdoor life, as well as other areas of life. (*Jonathan now looked in David and Priscilla's direction*) Thanks, Dad, and thanks, Mom, for teaching me how to be a well-rounded person.

David and Priscilla: (*in unison*) You are quite welcome; that is what good parents should do.

Ashley: (*now with a more solemn look on her face*) Now, back to the task at hand. As we look at each one of our selections, I think we can all agree, each one was based on the phonetic principle of sound. That is, we wrote down what we thought we heard. And as a result, we translated the sounds into what we thought to be the most familiar English word. Again, look at the three words I selected: *It's really real.*

Remember, each one of us has studied English and spoken it as our adopted language all our lives. And therefore, we are trained to formulate sounds in the English language. Furthermore, that is exactly what we are doing with the whip-poor-will (a bird) love song.

Again, remember I chose the three words: *It's really real.* First of all, I am intentionally going to focus on the word *really.* The first thing I want to do is define what part of speech the word 'really' is. The word 'really,' as used in my selection of words, is an adverb. It is a word that describes an adjective, a verb, or another adverb. Notice the three words I selected: *It's really real.* It describes the word *real.* Next, notice how the word *really* is pronounced by the whip-poor-will. It is my belief that it is pronounced with two syllables: *real-ly*, with stress on the first syllable.

The next word in my selection is *real*. Here, it is used as an adjective that describes a noun. One could ask at this juncture: What noun? Well, I purposefully noted this because to analyze the whip-poor-will love song, we need to answer this question: where is the noun? I will discuss this later. For now, let us continue analyzing the word *real*. Finally, I want to mention *real* is a two-syllable word: *re-al* (pronounced *ree-al*).

David, Priscilla, and Jonathan, as they listened to Ashley give them a *refresher course in English*, nodded with agreement, as they hung on to every observation Ashley made.

ASHLEY: (*with a sense of appreciation on her countenance*) Next, I want to talk about the first word I used in my selection: *It's really real.* The word *it's* is what I thought I heard. However, the more I think about it, I realize *it's* must be understood in terms of how it fits into my sentence. For example, what does the word *it's* mean?" (*now paused and looked at David, Priscilla, and Jonathan in an apologetic way*) I hope I am not sounding too *teachy.*

DAVID: (*with an encouraging smile on his face*) Please take your time because we all, with *bated breath*, are anxious to hear what you are saying. And by the way, I think we all sense where you are headed with your analysis. We believe it will be most beneficial to us in the final conclusion. And yes, it is wonderful to see how you are using your knowledge gained as an English major in college. Please continue. (*looking at Priscilla and Jonathan's direction, as they too nodded in agreement*)

ASHLEY: (*with a sense of satisfaction*) Thanks. Let us continue. Oh yes, we were talking about the word *It's*. What does *it's* mean? A better question to ask is when do we use *Its* instead of *It's*?

To answer this question, we need to, first of all, give a definition of each word: *Its* is a possessive form of the pronoun *it*, meaning belonging to it, whereas *It's* is a contraction of the words *it is.*

Remember, a contraction is a shortened form of a word or a group of words. In this sense, we use an apostrophe to represent the shortened form of the words *it is*.

With this in mind, I now think the words *It's really real* is a better choice than *Its really real*. Even so, we must remember the word *it* is a pronoun. And we recall we learned in grammar school a pronoun is a word used in place of a noun. Therefore, the question we have to answer is what is the noun *word* the whip-poor-will is referring to in its song?"

DAVID, PRISCILLA, and JONATHAN: (*suddenly, David, Priscilla, and Jonathan raised their hands and gave out loud applause*) Bravo, Ashley, for a job well done!

DAVID: It sounds like we all agree with your analysis and final selection of what you think the whip-poor-will is singing: "It's really real." Now let's make it official: How many *yeas* do we have? I count four hands. How many *nos* do we have? There are none. The vote is unanimous.

JONATHAN: (*walking over to Ashley and giving her a great big hug and a kiss, as he said in a somewhat hinting way*) Well done, teacher.

DAVID: (*immediately seized the moment by repeating the final question Ashley had asked in her presentation*) What is the noun *word* the whip-poor-will is referring to in its song?

To answer this question, it is my belief that what my father, Samuel, and my mother, Anne, said to me personally, in addition to what Mr. Bill, the wise old man, said during my interview and dialogue with him, gives us a strong lead in answering what noun *word* the whip-poor-will is using in its love song.

David expounds on what he heard his parents and Mr. Bill say about the whip-poor-will's love song

DAVID: I recall, as if it were just yesterday, my father and mother explaining how the whip-poor-will love song inspired them to be more loving toward God, their family, each other, and others in general. First of all, my parents explained to me what the Scriptures taught them about God. They reminded me that

God is love and that He is the source of love, that is, *agape* love. In addition, they reminded me God can use His creation to be conduits of His love. And they reminded me that God is using the whip-poor-will to convey to each other and to us a message of love.

I especially remember my mother using her experience as a teacher to explain the important ingredients of love: commitment, loyalty, giving, receiving, faithfulness, honor, and looking out for the well-being of the object of their love.

And finally, they indicated that, over the years, how the whip-poor-wills lived a life that showed a pattern of consistency. They indicated the whip-poor-wills' actions toward each other were consistent. They were consistent in how they supported each other as they worked together in meeting each other's needs. And how each played a mutual and shared role in raising and nurturing their offspring.

Most importantly, they showed us how consistent they were in being obedient to their calling and purpose in life. They were consistent in how they migrated further south to Central America, and South America during the winter season, returned to North America in spring, and remained throughout the summer.

Moreover, they were consistent in delivering the message of love to each other, and to us, beginning in early spring, and ending during the early autumn months. In essence, the whip-poor-wills' faithfulness in their actions toward one another showed them that what love does is a by-product of what love is.

David went on to say that over many years, he and Priscilla have had the privilege of watching the whip-poor-wills in action as they consistently sing with due diligence each night during spring and summer each year. Surely, it has reinforced their concept of love for God, for each other and their family, and for others.

DAVID: And yes, let us not forget that Mr. Bill, the wise old man, echoed this same sentiment as he underscored what had been observed by my parents, as well as by myself and Priscilla: God is using the whip-poor-will to sing a love song to each other, and to us! (*now pausing for a moment as he reflected on what he had said about the whip-poor-will and love. He now was ready to make his final point*) Here is my belief: the noun we are looking for is the word *love*. Therefore, let me suggest that the whip-poor-will love song goes like this: *My love for you, my love for you. It's really real. It's really real.* In other words, *love* is the *noun* we are looking for.

JONATHAN: (*after hearing his father make what will always be embedded in his memory, was now filled with an exuberant sense of excitement*) Eureka! Thanks, Dad, for helping us to solve the mystery.

PRISCILLA: (*now filled with tears of joy in her eyes, as she uttered with a sense of fulfillment*): Surely with this discovery, we have reached a key milestone in our search for the whip-poor-will love song. Indeed, it has already left an indelible imprint on all our lives, one that we will never forget. And now, it must be our mission to pass on this wonderful discovery to others for generations to come.

ASHLEY: (*reaching over and holding Jonathan's hand*) Indeed, I am sure that Jonathan will agree with me that our journey alongside David and Priscilla as we searched for the whip-poor-will love song leaves us no doubt about the real meaning of real love.

JONATHAN: (*as he held gently onto Ashley's hands and as he looked in his parents' direction*): Without a doubt, Dad and Mom, your example, and your leading in this journey in the search for the whip-poor-will love song, has indeed taught us what real love means. Thanks, Dad, and thanks, Mom, for helping Ashley and me not only understand what real love is but also exemplifying the role of real love itself. (*he could not hold it back any longer*) Let's go celebrate!

They went to their favorite restaurant and celebrated way into the night.

CHAPTER 12

Jonathan and Asley Are Now Convinced More than Ever that Their Love for Each Other Is Really Real

After having experienced the successful live recording of the whip-poor-will singing its love song, after listening to David and Priscilla explain how his father and mother had shared with him how the whip-poor-will faithfully, over many years, carried out their mission in raising their offspring, and faithfully singing their whip-poor-will love song throughout most of the night, from early spring to late summer of each year, and after the extensive dialogue and observation session that led them to unanimously agree that the whip-poor-will is singing about love, clearly, it was an experience Jonathan and Ashley would never forget, for they now knew the real meaning of love. They now knew that God is love. He is the giver of love, and He can use His creation, including the whip-poor-will, to be a conduit of His love.

As they discussed how to mutually express their love for each other in a way that would be a daily reminder of how much they love each other, more and more the whip-poor-will love song stood out in their mind. As a result, they both agreed they would call it "My Whip-Poor-Will Love Song."

Afterward, each one began comparing notes as to how they would word it in a way that would refer to how they love each other mutually.

As they pondered on this, they realized their parents, and yes, the whip-poor-will had already served as prime examples of how mutual love works. And most of all, they had learned that God is love and He is the source of true love, agape love. Note the wording of the song:

My Whip-poor-will Love Song

My love for you
My love for you
My love for you
It's really real…

Refrain: It's really real, it's really real, it's really real!
(Note: Used by permission, Charles Brookins Taylor Sr. 2023)

Jonathan and Ashley sing the whip-poor-will love song to each other

It was early June. The sea mist air of Long Island, New York, coming from the Long Island Sound on the north shoreside, clashed with the air from the Atlantic Ocean coming from the north shoreside. On this beautiful night, Jonathan and Ashley knew they needed to be alone. During their early years of dating, they had discovered a special inlet, a recessed area of the Atlantic Ocean near the house of Jonathan's parents where he grew up. They often went there to be alone.

On this particular evening, they carefully walked along a familiar sunbaked, foot-trodden path that led to their favorite spot. It was now in the late evening hours. As they looked westward, they could see the sun beginning to set, and as they looked eastward, they noticed the moon making its appearance.

They remembered the many times they used to gather up oyster shells, or even rock pellets, and throw them into the water to watch them skip and dance on the water's surface before finally sinking out of sight. On this special night, all was quiet except for the seagulls occasionally flying by.

As the sea mist air caressed their faces, they could feel its cooling effect like never before. As Jonathan and Ashley held each other's hands, they realized this was a special evening. It was a time to sing the whip-poor-will love song to each other. They had already discovered before that the inlet's water body mysteriously provided a special acoustical sound effect in a special way.

On this special occasion, they knew that they would be singing to God and to each other. As they joyfully sang to each other, they now knew beyond any doubt that their love for each other was really real. And now, more than ever, they were convinced that it was all because they had been blessed with parents and grandparents who, over the years, epitomized what real love means. And yes, they were very mindful that the whip-poor-will love song was a constant reminder of this very truth.

As Jonathan and Ashley held each other's hands, they sang the whip-poor-will love song to each other as tears of joy flowed from their eyes.

BOTH: (*with solemn looks on their faces as they were reading each other's minds*) It's time to call the preacher man.

CHAPTER 13

Jonathan and Ashley Meet with Pastor C. J. Richfield in a Counselling Session and to Schedule a Wedding Date

Pastor C. J. Richfield has served as the pastor of the church which Jonathan and his parents have been members of for many years. Ashley has attended there several times with Jonathan and his family. In fact, Pastor Richfield had the occasion to meet with Jonathan and Ashley several times before and was among the first to receive the news that they were engaged. And during which time, he had already spiritually discerned that they would soon be getting married.

Jonathan, over the years, had known other couples that were married by Pastor Richfield. Therefore, they were well aware that he only married couples after taking them through several required counseling sessions. In addition, they were aware he is also a certified premarital counselor, meaning that he was not only able to explain the biblical requirements for a Christian marriage but also what marriage means in terms of practical life experience.

Needless to say, he was well prepared for the occasion. So it goes without saying that they knew they had to be ready to answer questions as to the meaning of love and marriage and how they plan to live a lifelong marriage.

As they reflected back on their life experience of love, they were ever so grateful for what their parents had taught them about true love, that in the final analysis, love is what love does. And surely they could not forget how the whip-poor-will's life and love song has reinforced the real meaning of love. So Jonathan and Ashley felt they were well prepared for the counseling sessions.

Jonathan and Ashley meet with Pastor Richfield for premarital counseling

After the initial introductory protocol for the day, Pastor Richfield invited Jonathan and Ashley into the church's pastor's private office and study area. And after inviting them to sit in comfortable chairs on the opposite side of his desk, across from where he would be sitting, he looked toward them with a compassionate smile.

PASTOR RICHFIELD: I am ecstatic to hear that you all desire to get married. Remember, marriage is one of the most sacred institutions in our society: It is ordained by God. Therefore, it is one of the most important decisions in one's life.

Jonathan and Ashley nodded their heads in agreement. Pastor Richfield now looked at them with a compassionate and caring smile as he sensed they realized they were preparing to receive counseling that would help them to better understand the meaning and purpose of marriage and how to live out a successful marriage, one that would be blessed by God.

PASTOR RICHFIELD: First, let us look to God in prayer and ask Him to guide us in wisdom and truth as we participate in this very important counseling session.

Upon finishing his prayer, Pastor Richfield explained the purpose of premarital counseling. He indicated that Christian premarital counseling is the process of exploring each person's (man and woman) faith and history. The purpose is to help the couple to examine each other's personal convictions, and expectations for the future, and also, the responsibilities they will have along the way. And more than anything, premarital counseling's primary aim is to give the couple the skills and spiritual guidance that will help produce a marriage that is biblical and God-honoring.

PASTOR RICHFIELD: Jonathan, I am very much aware that you have been a member of this church since your youth days. Also, Ashley, I am pleased that you have attended here with Jonathan several times in the past. In fact, I was honored to meet with the two of you, informally several times before, and was pleased to hear that you all were engaged. (*looking at Jonathan and Ashley with a confirming smile on his face*) I have been looking forward to meeting with you to guide you through the steps that will prepare you for marriage. Before attempting to give you further instructions, I invite each one of you to tell me about your background. Jonathan, we will begin with you.

JONATHAN: (*taking a deep breath, as he began*) Pastor Richfield, I thank you for allowing us to meet with you for this occasion. In terms of my background, first, thanks to my parents who made sure I was exposed to a well-rounded life.

I was born and raised right here on Long Island, New York. I received Christ as my Savior at an early age, and have been a member of this Church all my life. And during most of my youth days, I followed the lead of my parents in attending Sunday school and Sunday morning worship service on a regular basis. However, during my late years in high school and as I started attending college, I must confess, like many other young people, my interest in attending church and studying the Scripture regularly became less and less. Again, like most young people, on an increasing basis, tend to become more independent in their way of thinking. And as a result, I tended to get involved in activities other than church activities.

And coupled with this, our colleges, by and large, do not emphasize the importance of Christian values. Instead, more emphasis is placed on humanism and what man can do for himself, apart from God.

Additionally, with the ever-changing cultural norms in our society, this, too, has influenced us, especially young people, to drift further away from God. But thanks to my parents. They would not let me forget the importance of remembering my Christian values and the foundation on which they stand.

It has been said that humans are imitative beings. From the cradle to the grave, we are learning to do and say what we see others say or do. I am very fortunate to have parents who serve as good role models in every aspect of their lives. And needless to say, they were consistent in living a God-honoring life before me, and in a loving way, they encouraged me to do likewise.

In addition, I am very fortunate to have been brought up in a home of a teacher and a social worker as parents. From my father, I was privileged to have the opportunity to learn much about biology, and science and their many related outdoor activities in practical ways, such as fishing, hunting, gardening, and bird-watching activities, just to name a few.

And, yes, my mother was a social worker. I thank my mother for sharing with me her experience of having to work with parents and young people who were less fortunate than we. Many of them did not have adequate resources to meet their everyday needs. I personally can remember how my mother and father would help support many of them in various ways. At the same time, they made sure I had the opportunity to participate in extracurricular activities, both at school and in our community.

And finally, I must say, I am sure my father has indicated to you he was born in Alabama, and how he and his family often traveled to Alabama to visit and explore the outdoor life of Alabama. One of his favorite pastimes is bird-watching, especially searching for the whip-poor-will and its love song. And need I say, I shall never forget that he and my mother made sure I was involved in their wonderful Alabama adventures.

In fact, they have given the charge to me, in taking the lead in extending our search of the whip-poor-will love song. And surely, it has influenced and inculcated in us a desire to do so with due diligence. My father and mother have retired and are planning on moving to Alabama soon, to live in retirement. I am sure they have already shared this information with you. (*Pastor Richfield nodded with a yes.*)

Meanwhile, for the time being, Ashley and I, after getting married, are planning on staying on Long Island, and begin raising a family here, at least for the time being. So this is a brief synopsis of my background, along with a brief look into the future.

Ashley gives a brief sketch of her background

ASHLEY: Pastor Richfield, I, too, want to express my gratitude to you for inviting Jonathan and me to attend your counseling session. In terms of my background, it is somewhat similar to Jonathan's in many aspects.

I was born and raised in what we call Upstate New York, in Middletown, New York, in the Hudson Valley Region, about seventy-one miles from New York City. It is essentially centered in a rural area. It is known for its New York State apples, its ciders, and its New York peaches. As is typical of most rural areas, most of us own and operate small farms.

So I, too, have been privileged with the opportunity to explore the many outdoor activities in our community and surrounding areas.

Many ask today: how do you keep from getting lonely in a small town such as yours? My answer to them would always be: there hardly ever is a dull moment for us because we consider the gardens, and for some of us, the small farm we had to manage, along with the animals we raised, as part of our extended family. So we had something to do 24-7, so to speak.

And now as I look back on my experience living on a farm, I realize it taught me the dignity of work. Both of my parents attended a Protestant church in our community and were faithful in their attendance and support.

Now as I look back on this experience, I am ever so grateful they were faithful in taking me and my siblings to church. At an early age, I accepted Christ as my Savior.

However, like Jonathan, as I grew into my late teens, I became more independent in my ways of thinking and began to allow other activities to interfere with my church attendance.

And yes, as Jonathan said earlier, upon entering college, I soon realized that our colleges do not emphasize the importance of Christian values. Rather, more emphasis is placed on humanism and what man can do for himself, apart from God.

Additionally, with this in mind, we must not forget, as Jonathan indicated earlier, that the ever-changing cultural norms in our society have led many young people to drift further and further away from God.

However, I credit my parents for their steadfast example as demonstrated in their life, the importance of maintaining a close relationship with God and daily studying His Word.

And I might add since I met Jonathan, and especially since our engagement, his parents have helped both of us to draw closer to God in our daily walk.

I shall forever be grateful to my parents for encouraging me to attend college here on Long Island. With their support and encouragement, I was blessed to graduate from college with a degree in English education, minoring in music and theater production.

And finally, as Jonathan indicated earlier, we plan to make Long Island our home and raise a family. (*now looking at Jonathan with a warm smile*) However, I am aware that Alabama and the whip-poor-will and its love song will always be in the back of our minds.

Pastor Richfield responds to what he has observed and heard Jonathan and Ashley say

PASTOR RICHFIELD: Thank you for sharing with me a brief autobiography of your life, in addition to giving me a preview of what you plan to do in the future. (*with a satisfying smile on his face*) You have made my job easier by sharing a brief sketch of your history: It is clear that the two of you have backgrounds that are very similar. It appears that you have a lot in common. Of course, you have already made me aware that you have known each other for almost four years and that you have been engaged to each other for one year. In addition, I am pleased to hear that you love the Lord and that you want Him to bless your marriage. In essence, you have already answered most of the questions I was prepared to ask you. However, something that stood out in your testimonies seems to indicate that the whip-poor-will love song has made a strong impact on your understanding of the meaning of love. And you, in particular, Jonathan, implied very strongly that your grandparents and your parents have shared with you that the whip-poor-will and its song, over many years, has also been a strong factor in how they viewed the meaning of love. Moreover, the thing that stood out for them is how consistent the whip-poor-wills have been in demonstrating that real love is love in action. This leads me to one of the important questions for both of you: Jonathan and Ashley: Do you love each other?

BOTH: (*looking at each other while holding hands, saying in unison with a solemn answer*) Yes, we do.

Jonathan seizes the moment to introduce the whip-poor-will love song that he and Ashley have mutually written together

Jonathan took the lead in asking Pastor Richfield's permission to sing the whip-poor-will love song to him.

PASTOR RICHFIELD: You not only have my permission, but it will be an honor to hear it!

Without any further hesitation, Jonathan and Ashley began singing the whip-poor-will love song:

My love for you,
My love for you,
My love for you,
It's really true.

My love for you,
My love for you,
My love for you,
It's really real.

Refrain: It's really real. It's really real. It's really real!

My love for you,
My love for you,
My love for you,
It's not just about how I feel.

My love for you,
My love for you,
My love for you,
It's the real deal.

My love for you,
My love for you,
The world didn't give it to me,
And the world can't take it from me.

My love for you,
My love for you,
God gave it to me,
My love for you will forever be.
My love for you,
My love for you,

It's like no other love,
For it comes from above.

Refrain: It's really real. It's really real. It's really real!

Like the whip-poor-will love song:
It's really real…

Upon hearing Jonathan and Ashley sing their whip-poor-will love song to each other, Pastor Richfield became so filled with overflowing joy, so much so, that he was almost speechless. After gaining his composure, he shouted out with his hands in the air.

PASTOR RICHFIELD: Glory to God! Glory to God! Thank you for that well-written and well-meaning song. And especially the way you two sing it with sincerity in your voices. (*with a slight pause*) May I share something with you about how God feels about the two of you?"

BOTH: (*with a grateful and accommodating smile, Jonathan and Ashley, as they looked at each other*), Sure, go right ahead, Pastor!

With the same beat and cadence that Jonathan and Ashley used in their whip-poor-will love song, Pastor Richfield began singing:

God's love for you,
God's love for you,
God's love for you,
It's really real.

God's love for you
God's love for you
God's love for you
It's really true.

God's love for you,
God's love for you,

The world didn't give it to you,
And the world can't take from you.

God's love for you,
God's love for you,
It's like no other love,
Because it comes from above.

Suddenly, Pastor Richfield realized he needed to continue leading Jonathan and Ashley through his counseling session.

PASTOR RICHFIELD: (*after pausing momentarily to catch his breath*) It is clear as a result of your testimonies within your individual autobiographies that you love the Lord, and you believe that God loves you. Of course, at this juncture I must ask you individually, do you love each other? (*looking in Jonathan's eyes*) Jonathan, do you love Ashley?

JONATHAN: (*now reached over and held Ashley by her hand and in a resounding way*) Yes, I love Ashley.

As Jonathan and Ashley continued to hold hands, Pastor Richfield now looked Ashley in her eyes.

PASTOR RICHFIELD: Ashley, do you love Jonathan?

ASHLEY: (*holding Jonathan's hand tighter*) Yes, I love Jonathan.

With a smile of satisfaction on his face, Pastor Richfield spoke with words of summation of the importance of love.

PASTOR RICHFIELD: You have just answered the three important questions about the importance of love: God loves you, you love God, and you love each other. Remember, God is love and, He is the source of unconditional love. And may you always remember that God desires that His love flow from Him, through you, to each other. And remember, too, His love is inexhaustible, like an eternal well, His well will never run dry. God's love is what holds our world together. And His love is the *glue* that will hold you and your family together.

(*after covering these key points as part of his counseling session*) I am confident that the two of you are well prepared to live a successful marriage. Finally, I will briefly mention other aspects of a marriage that will play important roles in your marriage: how you agree to handle your financial matters, how you agree to mutually share in home care activities, and how you agree to take the responsibility of encouraging each other to maintain a close relationship with God and the nurturing of your children in a Christian environment.

(*after discussing these and other key components that can help make a marriage a successful one, Pastor Richfield now with a smile of satisfaction on his face*) I believe I have covered all of the key points during my counseling session for the two of you. If there are no further questions or concerns you may have, I will now announce to you that you have successfully completed my counseling session with great satisfaction.

JONATHAN: Pastor Richfield, we thank you for this wonderful counseling session. (*as Ashley nodded in agreement*) It clearly will help Ashley and me to be better prepared for a successful marriage in the future. The question we now have is: where to from here?

A wedding date is set

With an accommodating smile on his face, Pastor Richfield realized that Jonathan's "where to from here" question was asked in a rhetorical sense. So Pastor answered by simply asking when would the two would like to set the wedding date. Again, Jonathan and Ashley held each other's hands, as Jonathan quickly reminded Pastor Richfield that he and Ashley had already discussed a wedding date after talking with a prospective wedding coordinator. She reminded us that normally a large wedding usually takes at least six months to arrange and coordinate all the items and activities to be included. After hearing this, Pastor Richfield, Jonathan, and Ashley agreed on the wedding date. However, he reminded them as they plan for their wedding, you would need to coordinate with him so that we can schedule at least one rehearsal session. And suddenly, a little voice within whispered to Pastor Richfield: "Suggest to them to sing their whip-poor-will love song at the wedding."

Jonathan and Ashley quickly acquiesced without hesitation. Ashley reminded Pastor Richfield that she and Jonathan had already discussed using the whip-poor-will love song during the wedding ceremony and for the wedding party afterward.

ASHLEY: By then we are hoping to have it arranged with musical notes.

Pastor Richfield (with a special smile on his face) was quick to remind Jonathan and Ashley that he was looking forward to officiating their marriage ceremony. After pausing for a moment, he reminded them that he felt the whip-poor-will love song would add a special meaning to their entire wedding ceremony. Jonathan nodded in agreement.

JONATHAN: True indeed. One thing is for sure, the whip-poor-will and its love song have played an important part in our search for the meaning of real love. Pastor Richfield, we will coordinate with you to schedule a rehearsal date.
PASTOR RICHFIELD: Very good.

He ended his counseling session with a prayer.

The wedding ceremony and the reception party were a success

Like any occasion of this magnitude, the planning for the wedding ceremony and its reception party required a lot of hard work. And indeed, their hard work was fruitful, for their wedding and the reception were filled with unforgettable memories they would never forget. Their family members and friends were in attendance for this happy occasion. And guess what? Everybody loved the whip-poor-will love song and wanted to know how they could obtain a copy of it.

CHAPTER 14

NOW THAT THE WEDDING CEREMONY IS OVER, AND NOW THAT THEIR HONEYMOON TRIP IS OVER, WHAT NOW?

Now that Jonathan and Ashley are married, the *what-now* questions began to pop up. First and foremost, they knew they needed to take time to reflect upon the primary influencers that gave them confidence in believing their marriage would be a successful one. Second, they were encouraged to hear how Jonathan's grandparents and parents shared with them how they credited the whip-poor-will and its love song, which they had observed during their lifetime, which reminded them, over and over again, of the whip-poor-will's consistency in singing the same love song from early spring to late summer, their consistency in supporting one another, and their consistency in how they raised their little birds during their growing stages of life. And most of all, how the whip-poor-wills' consistency in their faithfulness toward each other showed them that love is what it does. And most of all, they realized that their knowledge of how the Scriptures tells us God has ordained marriage and reminds us that it is God's love that enables husband and wife to have a successful marriage and live a successful life.

David and Priscilla, the parents of Jonathan, gave Jonathan and Ashley a final reminder before moving to Alabama

Before leaving New York to live in Alabama, David and Priscilla reminded Jonathan not to forget to continue to use the information that had been passed from his grandparents to David himself, and finally to Jonathan.

DAVID AND PRISCILLA: And most of all, remember the charge we gave: Take what you have learned about the whip-poor-will and its love song and pass it on to others and generations to come. Encourage others to take a cue from the whip-poor-will that shows us that all of God's creation, including the whip-poor-will, each of us, that is, human beings (the crown of God's creation), and each member of His creation. From the minutest of atoms to the largest sun, the tiniest amoeba to the greatest whale, and all things inestimable, in its own unique way, God has given them the ability to speak to us, each in its own language.

In essence, all of God's creation has been called on to proclaim the glory of God (Psalm 19:1). Although Jonathan and Ashley knew that their immediate business at hand was to settle into their family home and prepare to live life together as husband and wife. Yet they realized that the search for the whip-poor-will and its love song and its far-reaching meaning will be an ongoing endeavor in sharing it with others.

CHAPTER 15

What the Whip-poor-will and Its Love Song Teaches Us

First and foremost, the whip-poor-will and its love song have reminded us that God uses all of His creation in some form or fashion to proclaim His Glory. Humankind is the crown of God's creation; therefore, we are called on to take the lead in giving God the glory. However, one important thing to remember is that when we think of God's giving us the ability to give Him glory, it does not mean He created us so that He can become more glorious, that His beauty and perfection would be somehow increased by us. Nothing we do can take away or add to God's glory. For the glory of God is the beauty and excellence of His intrinsic and manifold perfections. Rather, He created us to display His glory, that is, that His glory might be known and praised. Toward this end, every part of creation is called on to proclaim God's glory. Things that we might think are not important or insignificant. For example, many do not view the whip-poor-will as important because it sleeps during the day and only sings at night. Or even that less than 1 percent of the world's population has ever seen one. And the few who have seen it, or even a picture of it, perceive it as being less attractive than most birds. Yet God is using the whip-poor-will as a special conduit to convey the message that God's love for us is really real. God has given the whip-poor-will a song to sing and a dance to dance, in its own language, in its own unique way. Likewise, He has given every part of His creation the ability to proclaim the glory of God, each in its own way, each in its own song, and each with its own dance. Listen to what the psalmist says in Psalm 148 (GNB) as he calls on the *whole universe to praise God*:

> Praise the Lord!
> Praise the Lord from heaven,
> You that live in the heights above.
>
> Praise him, all his angels,
> all his heavenly armies.
>
> Praise him, sun and moon;
> Praise him, shining stars.
>
> Praise him, highest heavens,
> and the waters above the sky.
>
> Let all praise the name of
> the LORD!
> He commanded, and they were
> created;
>
> By his command, they were fixed
> In their places forever,
> And they cannot disobey.
>
> Praise the Lord from the earth,
> sea monsters and all ocean depth;
>
> Lightning and hail, snow and clouds,
> strong winds that obey his commands.
>
> Praise him, hills and mountains,
> Fruit trees and forests;

All animals, tame and wild,
reptiles and birds.

Praise him, kings and all peoples,
princes and all other rulers:

Young women and young men,
old people and children too.

Let them all praise the name of
the Lord!

His name is greater than all others;
his glory is above earth and heaven.

He made his nation strong,

so that all his people praise him;
the people of Israel, so dear to him.

Praise the Lord! (Psalm 148:1–14 GNB).

And assuredly, each one of us who is born in the image of God and is the crown of His creation, is included in this clarion call, to proclaim His glory. Each one of us has been given the ability to praise Him and proclaim God's glory, each in his or her own language, each in his or her own song; each in his or her own dance. Quit letting the world tell you that you are not as important as others, or that you are an insignificant bystander. Quit having self-pity parties, or victimizing yourself. Rise up and use whatever gift (ability) God has given you to live out the true meaning and purpose of your life, by living and proclaiming the glory of God. Rise to the occasion that all of God's creation has been called to do. Join in the universal chorus of giving God the glory. When you allow this to happen, when you join the universal chorus of praising God and giving Him the glory, your life will begin to have a purpose; your life will become filled with peace, happiness, and joy! This is what the whip-poor-will and its love song is teaching us in its own language, in its own unique way when it sings each night, during the early spring and throughout the late summer nights: "God's love for you; it's really real, it's really real, it's really real!"